Study Guide

INTRODUCTORY FINANCIAL ACCOUNTING

Judith Ramaglia
PACIFIC LUTHERAN UNIVERSITY

Study Guide
INTRODUCTORY FINANCIAL ACCOUNTING
Third Edition

Gerard G. Mueller
UNIVERSITY OF WASHINGTON
and
Lauren Kelly
UNIVERSITY OF WASHINGTON

 Prentice Hall, Englewood Cliffs, New Jersey 07632

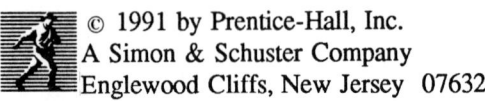
Printed in the United States of America

10 9 8 7 6 5 4 3 2

ISBN 0-13-485871-9

Prentice-Hall International (UK) Limited, *London*
Prentice-Hall of Australia Pty. Limited, *Sydney*
Prentice-Hall Canada Inc., *Toronto*
Prentice-Hall Hispanoamericana, S.A., *Mexico*
Prentice-Hall of India Private Limited, *New Delhi*
Prentice-Hall of Japan, Inc., *Tokyo*
Simon & Schuster Asia Pte. Ltd., *Singapore*
Editora Prentice-Hall do Brasil, Ltda., *Rio de Janeiro*

CONTENTS

PREFACE

This STUDY GUIDE was designed to supplement Mueller and Kelly's INTRODUCTORY FINANCIAL ACCOUNTING. The intent is to improve your comprehension and retention of the material. Each chapter of the text is outlined in the STUDY GUIDE. You may find it useful to scan the appropriate outline before you begin reading the related chapter in the text to give you a preview of the content. Obviously, the outlines can also be used for review. The STUDY GUIDE also provides sets of objective questions (primarily true/false and multiple choice) for each of the chapters in the text. The coverage is comprehensive, and includes items related to the content of the Appendix to Chapter Five. The questions cover both conceptual and procedural matters.

Note that it is possible to test extensive, integrated processes (preparation of the Statement of Cash Flows, Price Level Adjustments, the accounting information cycle, and so forth) with objective questions. This is done with sets of questions which must be answered by reference to a single data base. For example, in the material for Chapter Three, questions 70-77 are all based on the information for a single month of a company's operations. This approach is repeated in the other chapters. For example, in the material for Chapter Five, even though questions 26-39 appear as individual items, you are, in effect, preparing a complete Statement of Cash Flows for the Belved Company. All you would need to do is organize your answers to the individual questions in the format for a Statement of Cash Flows.

ACKNOWLEDGEMENT

I wish to thank Professor Gerhard Mueller and Professor Lauren Kelly for their support and encouragement.

Over the years many of the accounting faculty at the University of Washington have contributed to the test file for the course in which this text is used. As I have drawn freely from that file, I wish to acknowledge the contributions of those faculty. Any errors are, of course, my own responsibility.

Study Guide
INTRODUCTORY FINANCIAL ACCOUNTING

CHAPTER ONE

THE ROLE OF ACCOUNTING

CHAPTER OUTLINE

A. WHAT IS ACCOUNTING, AND HOW IS IT USED?

1. Accounting is the language of business.

2. The purpose of accounting is to provide quantitative information about economic entities that is useful in making economic decisions.

3. Information is knowledge that is helpful in reaching a conclusion.

4. Economic entities include individuals, business enterprises, nonbusiness organizations, social programs, and units of government.

5. Accounting information about these economic entities is used in a wide variety of situations.

B. WHAT IS FINANCIAL ACCOUNTING?

1. Financial accounting is limited to business enterprises and external users.

2. External users are persons making decisions related to the entity even though they are not employed by the entity to direct its activities or utilize its resources. These include investors, suppliers, taxing authorities, and so forth.

3. Financial accounting is used by external parties to make decisions

related to business enterprises.

4. A business enterprise is an organization comprised of one or more individuals, capital goods, and other resources, whose purpose is to produce specific products or services for sale.

C. HOW ARE DECISIONS MADE ?

1. Society has virtually unlimited wants and needs but limited resources.

2. Resources include: <u>land</u> (or natural resources), <u>labor</u> (mental or physical), <u>capital</u> (implements, technologies, learned techniques for increasing the output of our resources), and <u>entrepreneurial ability</u>.

3. To solve the conflict between unlimited wants or needs and limited resources, members of society are continually making decisions.

4. Decision making is the process of choosing from among alternative courses of action using criteria adopted by the decision maker.

5. Decision making can be modeled as a seven-stage process: a need is felt, the problem is identified, information is sought about alternatives, the alternatives are evaluated, a conclusion is reached or an action selected, an action is taken (if appropriate), the outcome is reviewed.

6. Identifying the problem involves establishing objectives and determining constraints.

7. In seeking information about alternatives the decision maker wants to reduce uncertainty, that is, to improve predictions of the outcomes of uncertain future events.

8. Information is relevant with respect to a specific decision if it will improve predictions regarding future events related to the decision.

9. Decision making is NOT choosing the most desirable alternative; it is the process of finding the best combination of the expected outcome and the amount of resources which must be spent.

10. When large numbers of individuals make decisions involving similar courses of action, there is a need for information specialists.

11. Information specialists are individuals who devote resources to producing decision-relevant information for use by others.

12. Information specialists can provide information at a lower cost than would be incurred by others individually gathering the same facts.

13. Accountants are information specialists who enable the functioning of the economy.

D. WHAT IS THE NATURE OF BUSINESS ENTITIES?

1. To study the information needed by decision makers concerned with business entities, it is necessary to understand the role of the business enterprise.

2. Entrepreneurs are people who provide products and services in response to demand by potential customers.

3. These individuals organize factors of production (labor, capital) to produce goods and services and take the risk that the price they get will not exceed the costs of the factors.

4. In their organizing and risk taking entrepreneurs usually structure themselves as a business enterprise.

5. A business enterprise is an organization comprised of one or more individuals, capital goods, and other resources, whose purpose is to produce specific products or services for sale.

6. The business enterprise is a means of coordinating the activities of individuals engaged in production processes.

7. The business enterprise is also a means of sharing among many individuals the enterprise function by obtaining funds to finance the workings of the business.

8. Entrepreneurs who see profit opportunities may not have sufficient money capital to exploit those opportunities; thus, they may borrow money in exchange for fixed interest payments or arrange for others to share ownership of the enterprise.

9. The business enterprise is a means of breaking down a large profit opportunity into a number of smaller individual opportunities.

10. The three traditional kinds of business enterprises are: proprietorships, partnerships, and corporations.

11. The proprietorship
    a. is recognized as a separate accounting entity;
    b. is not a separate legal entity;
    c. puts all of the proprietor's personal wealth at risk;
    d. may be dissolved at will;
    e. is dissolved automatically upon the death of the proprietor.

12. Partnerships
    a. are recognized as separate accounting entities;
    b. are not separate legal entities;
    c. put all of a least one partner's personal wealth at risk;
    d. are dissolved upon the death, withdrawal or bankruptcy of any partner;
    e. usually do not permit a partner to transfer (sell) his interest without the consent of the other partner(s).

13. Corporations
    a. are separate accounting entities
    b. are separate legal entities;
    c. render shareholders' liability limited to their ownership share of the resources and profits of the corporation.
    d. do not permit the owners (stockholders) to directly conduct the business;
    e. do not permit the owners to directly use its resources;
    f. do not permit the owners to bind it by their actions;
    g. grant the stockholders the right to vote for directors;
    h. grant the stockholders the right to share in the profits of the corporation;
    i. give owners the right to sell their shares without consent of the other stockholders;
    j. have indefinite lives.

E. WHAT COMMON TYPES OF DECISIONS ARE MADE REGARDING BUSINESS ENTITIES ?

1. Two classes of decision makers are concerned with the business enterprise: internal and external.

2. Managerial accounting focuses on the needs of internal users; financial accounting focuses on the needs of external users.

3. Internal users include managers and other employees. They are concerned with choosing among alternatives available to the business enterprise.

4. External users include investors, creditors, suppliers, etc. They view the business enterprise as one decision alternative available to themselves personally.

5. The _external_ user is interested in two types of decisions:
   a. individual investment decisions and
   b. decisions about the distribution of enterprise benefits.

6. An individual's investment decision involves an exchange of present resources for rights to resources in the future.

7. Investors in a business are its creditors and owners.

8. Investors may acquire the rights of creditors or owners either by buying them directly from the business or by buying the transferable rights of present creditors and owners.

9. Generally, a creditor receives from the business a contractual obligation:

   a. to pay a specified amount of money (the principal) after a specified time interval and
   b. to pay periodically a specified amount (rate of interest) on the principal.

10. An owner receives ownership interest in all rights and properties owned by the business in proportion to his or her ownership percentage.

11. The owner also receives the right to share proportionally in distributed profits of the business (dividends) and the firm's resources if the entity ceases to exist.

12. Owners are residual beneficiaries. After all existing claims against a company have been satisfied, the owners possess the remaining properties and rights.

QUESTIONS AND EXERCISES

TRUE-FALSE. Indicate whether each of the following statements is true or false.

_____1-1. Accounting provides information for decision-making by individuals, business enterprises, social organizations, and governments.

_____1-2. <u>Financial</u> accounting is used by external parties to make decisions related to business enterprises, social programs, and units of government.

_____1-3. Decision making is the process of choosing from among alternative courses of action using criteria adopted by the decision maker.

_____1-4. A business enterprise provides a means for coordinating the activities of individuals engaged in large-scale production with a high degree of division or labor and specialization.

_____1-5. One of the advantages of a sole proprietorship is that it is a separate legal entity, independent of its owner(s).

_____1-6. One of the advantages of a corporation is that it is a separate legal entity, independent of its owner(s).

_____1-7. Generally, owners of stock can sell their shares of stock without the consent of other shareholders.

_____1-8. Owners (stockholders) receive the rights to share proportionally in the distributed profits of the enterprise.

_____1-9. A creditor receives the right to periodic interest payments.

_____1-10. Residual beneficiaries are parties whose rights and claims remain after all existing statutory and contractual rights and claims have been satisfied.

_____1-11. The need for economic decisions arises because society must allocate unlimited resources to limited wants and needs.

6

___1-12. Money capital is the cash (or cash equivalent of other resources) committed to a business enterprise to enable it to procure and meet its obligations to pay for capital goods, labor, material, and so forth.

___1-13. Creditors are the residual beneficiaries of a business entity.

___1-14. In a market economy it is the potential for profit that motivates the production of goods and services.

___1-15. In decision making more data is always preferred to less.

MATCHING. Complete each statement by filling in the blanks with the letter corresponding to the most appropriate term selected from the list below.

a.	decision relevance	b.	accounting entity
c.	internal user	d.	accounting
e.	financial accounting	f.	uncertainty
g.	information	h.	information specialist
i.	business enterprise	j.	external user
k.	decision making		

1-16. An accountant is also known as a(n) _____.

1-17. _____improves the expected outcome of a decision.

1-18. _____provides quantitative information about economic entities to help the user in making economic decisions.

1-19. A(n) _____is made up of one or more individuals, capital goods, and a purpose.

1-20. A(n) _____is interested in choosing among decision alternatives available to the business enterprise itself.

1-21. Information that will improve the predictions of the outcomes of future events is said to possess more_____.

1-22. The branch of accounting designed for external groups is _____.

1-23. The process of choosing among alternative courses of action is _____.

1-24. A(n) _____ views a business enterprise as one decision alternative or opportunity available to herself.

<u>MULTIPLE-CHOICE. - Select the best response for each of the following, and mark the letter corresponding to your choice.</u>

1-25. The most significant role of accounting is to

    a. Measure the performance of business and government managers.
    b. Prepare financial statements.
    c. Measure wealth.
    d. Facilitate economic decisions.

1-26. A corporation

    a. Places the entire personal wealth of the owner(s) at risk.
    b. Is a separate legal entity.
    c. Is generally characterized by easy transferability of ownership.
    d. a and b
    e. b and c

1-27. When making a decision all available information is usually not gathered before selecting from the available alternatives because

    a. There are limits to a person's ability to process large amounts of information.
    b. The benefits of gathering additional information may be exceeded by its costs.
    c. Since it is not possible to know the future with certainty, there is no point in gathering much information.
    d. All of the above are correct.
    e. a and b are correct.

1-28. An accounting entity

    a. Is involved in using economic resources to achieve a purpose.
    b. Has an identity of its own.
    c. Is of interest to one or more individuals for decision-making purposes.
    d. Only b and c are correct.
    e. All of the above are correct.

1-29. In a market economy, entrepreneurs

    a. Serve to recognize opportunities to profit from production of goods or services.
    b. Serve to organize the resources to exploit profit opportunities.
    c. Provide all the capital necessary to exploit profit opportunities.
    d. Only a and b are correct.
    e. All of the above are correct.

1-30. Which of the following is considered to be an accounting entity ?

    a. Proprietorship.
    b. Partnership.
    c. Corporation.
    d. U.S. Government.
    e. All of the above are considered to be accounting entities.

1-31. What is a key difference between corporations and partnerships?

    a. Corporations may own other corporations; partnerships may not own corporations.
    b. Partnerships must have fewer than twenty owners; corporations may have any number of owners.
    c. Limited liability applies to the owners of corporations, whereas unlimited liability applies to owners of partnerships.
    d. Partnerships are separate legal entities; corporations are not separate legal entities.

1-32. Consider a decision problem relating to what kind of crops to plant on a tract of land. In a decision theory context, the fact that average rainfall in the area is twenty-five inches per year would be an example of:

    a. A statement of objectives.
    b. A constraint.
    c. An alternative action.
    d. All of the above.
    e. None of the above.

1-33. In the decision making process the step that follows the review of the action taken is:

a. A felt need is recognized.
b. Problem identification.
c. Determination of alternatives.
d. Evaluation of alternatives.
e. Selection of best alternative.

1-34. Decision making is defined as the process of choosing among alternative courses of action according to some criteria adopted by the decision maker. Therefore,

a. The decision maker must obtain information prior to making a decision.
b. Once decision criteria are specified, they cannot be changed with respect to the decision to be made.
c. In the decision making process, alternative courses of action are evaluated before the problem is identified.
d. Uncertainty is an element of decision making; with enough information one can eliminate uncertainty.
e. None of the above.

1-35. Which one of the following is not usually considered an external user of financial accounting information?

a. Banker.
b. Supplier.
c. Absentee owner.
d. Department manager.
e. Internal Revenue Service.

CHAPTER TWO

PRESENT VALUE APPROACH
TO INVESTMENT DECISIONS

CHAPTER OUTLINE

A. THE INVESTMENT DECISION PROBLEM

1. The objective of investment decisions is to increase one's wealth.

2. Wealth is the command over present and future goods and services owned or controlled by an economic unit at a point in time.

3. Investment decisions involve exchanging present goods/services for rights to future goods/services.

4. To evaluate investments the decision maker must be able to measure the present wealth sacrificed and the wealth expected in return.

5. Assume that all investment alternatives are composed exclusively of cash flows.

6. Investment alternatives differ only with regard to the magnitude and the timing of the cash flows

7. The decision maker must decide which set of cash flows is "better."

B. THE PRESENT VALUE DECISION MODEL

1. An individual's preference for a given amount of money now, rather than the same amount at some future time, is called time preference for money.

2. Time preference for money can be expressed as an interest rate. This is the point at which an individual is indifferent between two alternatives.

3. The time preference rate is also called the "discount rate".

4. This rate helps individuals to evaluate investment alternatives.

5. Individuals use the rate to translate different amounts of cash flowing at different points in time to equivalent amounts of value at the present.

6. An individual's time preference rate is affected by (a) the present level of consumption enjoyed and (b) the attractiveness of opportunities available.

7. An investor's opportunity rate is the rate that can be earned on the best known investment alternative. The investor's time preference rate is equivalent to his or her opportunity rate.

8. The time preference rate can be used to determine what amounts would induce an individual to postpone possession of cash. For example, if an individual has a time preference rate of ten percent, she would be indifferent between

    (a) receiving a specific amount of cash today or

    (b) accepting an equivalent amount plus a ten percent compounded return on that amount at some point in the future.

9. The future value (FV) of one dollar at a specified interest rate (r) for a given number of periods (n) is equal to:

$$FV = \$1 \ X \ (1.0 + r)^n$$

10. This can be used to compute the amount an individual would have to receive at some point in the future in order to be

induced to forego cash in the present.

11. It is often more appropriate in investment decisions to work from future cash flows to their present values.

12. The present value of a future cash flow is the amount of current cash that leaves a decision maker indifferent between it and a specified amount of cash to be received or paid at a future date.

13. The present value of one dollar at a specified interest rate (r) for a given number of periods (n) is equal to:

$$PV = \$1 \ X \ \frac{1}{(1.0 + r)^n}$$

14. Present value arithmetic is the reciprocal of future value arithmetic.

15. An annuity is a series of periodic future cash flows identical as to their amount.

16. The present value of an annuity can be determined by summing the present value factors and multiplying the total by the periodic cash flow.

C. THE NET PRESENT VALUE DECISION MODEL

1. Specify the amount and time of occurrence of cash inflows and outflows.

2. Calculate the present value of each individual cash inflow and outflow.

3. Sum the present values of all the positive and all the negative cash flows.

4. Find the net present value by calculating the difference between the total present value of the positive cash flows and the total present value of the negative cash flows.

5. If only one alternative is to be selected, choose the one with the highest net present value.

6. If the decision maker can select more than one alternative, she should make all investments with a positive net present value until her investment funds expire.

D. PRESENT VALUE, WEALTH, AND INCOME

1. Wealth is the command over present and future goods and services owned or controlled by an economic unit as of a point in time.

2. Investment decisions are exchanges of present goods or services for rights to goods or services in the future.

3. When investment decisions lead to greater quantities of goods or services in the future (assessed at their present value), wealth is increased.

4. In the context of the net present value model wealth is measured as current cash on hand plus the present value of the future cash inflows and outflows to be received from all noncash wealth items.

5. Valuation is the measurement of wealth in money terms.

6. The net present value of an investment opportunity may be thought of as the improvement in wealth that will result from selecting an investment opportunity.

7. For an individual investor, income is the increase in wealth that occurs during a period of time.

8. If wealth is defined in present value terms, income is the change in the present value of the investment that occurs over time.

E. CAVEATS

1. The outcome of a decision can be highly sensitive to the time preference rate selected.

2. Uncertainty is involved at each stage of the decision process. Under uncertainty the best the decision maker can do is to choose the alternative that is expected to provide the greatest satisfaction.

3. The role of financial accounting is to assist the external decision maker in projecting expected cash inflows and outflows from alternative investments.

QUESTIONS AND EXERCISES

Matching. Match the term to its definition.

A. Wealth   B. Opportunity rate
C. Present value   D. Future value
E. Net present value   F. Time preference for money

____2-1. That which can be earned on the best-known investment alternative.

____2-2. The amount of current cash that leaves a decision maker indifferent between it and a specified amount of cash to be received or paid at a future date.

____2-3. The amount of future cash that leaves a decision maker indifferent between it and a specified amount of cash to be received or paid currently.

____2-4. Command over present and future goods and services.

____2-5. An individual's preference for a given amount of money now, rather than the same amount at some future time.

____2-6. The sum of the present values of the future cash inflows minus the sum of the present values of the future cash outflows of an investment opportunity.

15

2-7. On the day of a child's birth, the parents deposited $1,000 in an account. How much will it be worth on the child's eighteenth birthday, assuming an interest rate of ten percent?

 a. $2,800
 b. $8,200
 c. $5,560
 d. None of the above.

2-8. At the end of each year a company put $40,000 in a special account. How much will it be worth at the end of three years, assuming a discount rate of ten percent?

 a. $128,000
 b. $132,400
 c. $132,000
 d. None of the above.

2-9. What will be the value three years from now of an investment of $4,000 now and $4,000 one year from now if your time preference rate is 12% ?

 a. $6,036.
 b. $9,480.
 c. $9,600.
 d. $10,600.

2-10. What is the present value of a $30,000 payment to be received in five years, assuming a time preference rate of ten percent?

 a. $18,630
 b. $48,300
 c. $15,000
 d. $113,700

2-11.   If the opportunity rate is seven percent, what is the future value
        of $2,000 four years from today ?

        a. $1,526
        b. $6,780
        c. $2,560
        d. $2,620

2-12.   If the discount rate is nine percent, what is the present
        value of $3,000 to be received in six years ?

        a. $5,040
        b. $1,641
        c. $1,380
        d. $1,788

2-13.   I have a 12% discount rate, and an opportunity to invest
        $2,000 in order to receive an annuity of $200 at the end of
        each of the next twelve months.

        a. I will take the opportunity as its net present value is $252.
        b. I will not take the opportunity as its net present value is -$762.
        c. I will take the opportunity as its net present value is $1,238.
        d. I will take the opportunity as its net present value is $2,252.

2-14.   If an investment opportunity has the following cash
        inflows and outflows, what is its net present value at a
        discount rate of 6%?

                                           YEAR

                        0   1   2   3   4

        Inflow   --- $200 $900 $650 $475
        Outflow $100 $200 $800 $550 $375

        a. $152.20.
        b. $252.20
        c. $167.00
        d. $347.00
        e. None of the above.

2-15. You have decided to purchase a new machine and have been given two options:
1. Four annual payments of $5,000 each, the first payment due when the machine is picked up, i.e., at time "0".
2. An unspecified lump sum purchase price.
If your time preference rate is 14%, what would you be willing to pay if you elected the lump sum purchase option?

a. $20,000.
b. $14,550.
c. $16,600.
d. $17,250.

2-16. You are considering the purchase of Evergreen Stock. Each share of stock costs $47 and you would like to buy ten shares. You expect Evergreen to pay dividends of $2 per share at the end of each year you own the stock. You only want to invest for five years. What is the MINIMUM amount per share you would have to sell the stock for at the end of five years to make this a wise investment? Your time preference rate is ten percent.

a. $63.48
b. $37.00
c. $10.40
d. $65.67
e. None of the above.

2-17. What is the effect on the net present value (NPV) of an investment of decreasing the discount rate applied to the cash flows?

a. The NPV becomes smaller.
b. The NPV is unchanged.
c. The NPV becomes larger.
d. It is not possible to determine the effect without the actual data.
e. None of the above.

2-18. Suppose you had the opportunity to invest $1,000 at 15%. For approximately how many years would you have to invest the money to double it?

a. 3 years.
b. 5 years.
c. 8 years.
d. 10 years.
e. It is impossible to tell with the information given.

2-19.   You have just won "$1,000,000" in the State Lottery. You will receive
        twenty equal annual payments of $50,000. You wonder what the
        present value of the twenty equal payments is as of today, keeping in
        mind that the state will withhold 20% of each payment for federal
        income taxes. The best rate at which you can invest these funds is
        10%. You intend to pick up the first check this afternoon. The
        present value of your "million dollar prize" is:

        a. $334,800.
        b. $334,400.
        c. $350,400.
        d. $374,400

2-20.   Anticipating the future receipt of $1,000, you look up the
        appropriate table factor in "future-value of a single amount"
        table, write down "2.10" and calculate what you think to be a
        present value. Sometime later, when the tables are no longer
        available, you realize your error. Based on this information
        alone, what is the present value of the $1,000?

        a. $1,000 X (2.10 ÷ 1,000).
        b. (2.10 ÷ 1) X $1,000.
        c. $1,000 ÷ 2.10.
        d. (1 + 2.10) X $1,000.

2-21.   A corporation issues a bond that contracts to pay the purchaser
        $20,000 every six months for three years and to pay a $500,000
        principal amount (face value) at the end of the three year period.
        How much should an investor with a ten percent time preference
        rate be willing to pay for the bond ?

        a. $474,600
        b. $620,000
        c. $464,000
        d. $495,200

19

2-22. The Helping Hand Loan Company placed an advertisement in a local newspaper that read, in part, "Borrow up to $10,000 for five years at our low, low rate of interest of six percent per year." When a customer went to the loan company to borrow $10,000, he was told that total interest on the five-year loan would be $3,000; that is, $600 per year (six percent of $10,000) for five years. Company practice, he was told, required that interest be paid in full at the time a loan is made and be deducted from the amount given to the customer. Thus, the customer was given $7,000. The loan was to be repaid in annual installments of $2,000. What was the approximate rate of interest the borrower was really paying on this loan?

a. 6%
b. 10%
c. 20%
d. 13%

2-23. Mr. Smith wishes to buy a ten-year annuity. He has available $10,000 to spend. Approximately what amount should he expect to receive at the end of each of the ten years, if his opportunity rate is ten percent?

a. $1,629
b. $614
c. $6,140
d. $61,400

2-24. As a result of the excellent grades you received last quarter, your rich grandparents sent you a check for $1,000 which you received and deposited in your bank on January 2, 1991. To what amount will that deposit grow to in three years if your bank pays eight percent interest compounded quarterly?

a. $1,060
b. $1,260
c. $1,270
d. $2,520

2-25.   You have been given several investment opportunities to analyze and are comfortable with the projected cash inflows and outflows. You are not comfortable with the opportunity rate needed to complete your calculations, since interest rates seem to vary widely. If you decide to use the same inflows/outflows but use a high and low opportunity rate in your analysis, which rate will produce the most favorable net present value?

a. The highest one.
b. The lowest one.
c. Both rates will produce the same answer.
d. More information is needed to answer the question.

2-26.   Mr. Wilson buys an automobile. He pays cash of $1,000 immediately and agrees to pay the balance in four annual installments of $1,000. The first installment is due one year after the purchase date. What is the "cash price" of the automobile (i.e., the price if Mr. Wilson paid in full at the time of purchase) ? Assume an interest rate of 10%.

a. $5,000
b. $4,500
c. $4,170
d. $4,545

CHAPTER THREE

BASIC CONCEPTS AND INCOME DETERMINATION

CHAPTER OUTLINE

A. INFORMATION FOR MAKING INVESTMENT DECISIONS.

1. Future cash flows to the investor must be predicted before the present value decision model can be used.

2. Unless the enterprise generates cash in the future, it will be unable to distribute cash to its investors.

3. Creditors rely on the firm to have cash to pay the interest due and repay the principal.

4. Owners rely on the firm to have cash to pay dividends.

5. Potential investors' expectations regarding the firm's profitability and future cash available for dividends determine stock prices.

6. Future cash flows expected by the firm enable investors to predict the amounts and probabilities of the cash payments the firm will make to them as creditors or owners.

7. Since they are external to the firm, it is difficult for investors to generate forecasts of a firm's future cash flows.

8. Management may be reluctant to make forecasts of future cash flows available to the public, as such information could be used against them by their competitors; it could also be inaccurate.

9. An alternative information base would be historical cash flows, or the cash basis of accounting.

B. CASH BASIS.

1. The firm's cash receipts and disbursements for a time period are measured to determine the firm's performance.

2. This evaluation of past performance is then used to predict future cash flows.

3. Cash basis accounting includes all sources and uses of cash, whether from outside investors or business operations.

4. Net operating cash flow excludes
   a. cash receipts from owners;
   b. cash receipts from long-term creditors;
   c. cash paid for dividends or withdrawals paid to owners;
   d. cash used for repayment of long-term debt.

5. Historical cash flow information is factual; it is not based on estimates.

6. Current period net operating cash flow is a measure similar to the future period cash flow information that is of interest to investors.

7. When measured over short periods of time, net operating cash flow may seriously misrepresent the long-run cash-generating ability of the firm.

8. There is no necessary association between the measure of effort (total cash expenditures) and the measure of accomplishment (total cash receipts).

9. For example, buying a piece of equipment may be good for future cash generating ability, but it will have a negative effect on the current period's net operating cash flow.

10. Because it depends on erratic cash flows this cash flow measure does not provide information which is adequate for predicting future performance.

C. ACCRUAL BASIS.

1. The accrual basis of accounting was developed as a measurement procedure intended to associate the positive and negative aspects of operations with the appropriate time period.

2. The object of this procedure is to recognize the financial effects of transactions and events on the firm in the period in which they are experienced by the entity.

3. Using accrual accounting to measure a firm's performance results in the determination of income.

4. Income is the accounting measure of the firm's change in wealth.

5. Revenues are used to measure a firm's periodic accomplishments.

6. Revenues are actual and/or expected cash inflows during a period from delivering or producing goods, rendering services, or other activities that represent the entity's business purpose.

7. Revenues include both cash and credit sales.

8. Revenues exclude cash receipts in the current period which represent payments made by customers for products/services received in an earlier period.

9. Measuring revenue is subjective in that one must determine the time period when the enterprise provides the goods or services.

10. Revenue has been realized when goods or services are exchanged for cash or claims to cash; generally, this is when

    (a) the prices to be received for the products/services become reasonably certain and
    (b) the prices have been earned by the firm.

11. "Earned" means that the firm does not face any substantial additional production barriers or steps, such as delivery.

12. Recognition is the process of recording or including the financial measurement of a transaction, event, or circumstance in the firm's

measure of current period performance.

13. Over the whole life of the enterprise, the sum of all periods' revenues will equal the sum of all periods' cash receipts from sales of products and services.

14. Differences between the <u>revenue</u> and the <u>cash receipts</u> of a firm are almost always <u>a matter of timing.</u>

15. <u>Expenses</u> are the measure of a firm's periodic effort or sacrifice.

16. <u>Expenses</u> are the outflows or costs of resources during a period used to deliver or produce goods, render services, or carry out other activities that <u>represent the entity's business purpose.</u>

17. Expenses are actual or expected cash outflows that have or will occur in order to produce the current period's revenue.

18. <u>Matching</u> is the process of including the expenses incurred to produce and sell a product or service in the same time period as the revenues they generated.

19. Determining the <u>revenues</u> realized <u>precedes</u> identifying the <u>expenses</u> to be recognized in any given time period.

20. Matching requires that every resource used in production in a given period

    (a) be specifically identified with a particular product or service,
    (b) have its cost added with the costs of all other resources used to produce that product or service, and
    (c) be recognized as an expense in the period in which that product or service is sold.

21. <u>Product expenses</u> are resource costs that logically attach to products; product costs are recognized as expenses in the period in which the particular product is sold.

22. <u>Period expenses</u> relate more closely to specific time periods than to an identifiable product or service.

23. Subtracting the expenses incurred from the revenue earned in a specific time period yields the firm's income.
    (Revenues - Expenses = Income)

24. The firm's income is its increase in wealth over a period of time.

25. Income measurement is essential information for the investor to be able to predict future returns from being a creditor or owner.

26. Gains (losses) are inflows (outflows) of resources from transactions and other events and circumstances which affect the entity during a period but are incidentally related to the entity's business purpose.

27. Extraordinary gains and losses are **both**

    (a) highly infrequent and
    (b) unusual.

28. **Income or loss from continuing operations** is the difference between revenues from operations and related expenses, plus or minus gains or losses, for a given period of time.

       Revenues
    - Expenses
    + Gains
    - Losses
    Income from continuing operations

29. **Net income or loss** is income or loss from continuing operations plus or minus extraordinary gains or losses.

       Revenues
    - Expenses
    + Gains
    - Losses
    Income from continuing operations
    + Extraordinary gains
    - Extraordinary losses
    NET INCOME

QUESTIONS AND EXERCISES

MATCHING. Complete each statement by filling the blanks with the letter of the most appropriate term selected from the list below.

a. revenue
b. realization
c. matching
d. net operating cash flow
e. recognition
f. net income
g. income from continuing operations

h. expenses
i. accrual
j. cash
k. product expenses
l. period expenses
m. gains and losses
n. extraordinary items

____3-1. The basis of accounting that reports the entity's cash receipts and cash disbursements during a specific time period.

____3-2. The excess of total cash received by the enterprise during a period of time over total cash disbursed during the same period of time, excluding dividends or withdrawals paid to owners, repayment of long-term debt, or cash receipts from owners or long-term creditors.

____3-3. Accounting that records the financial effects on an enterprise of transactions and other events and circumstances that have cash consequences for the enterprise in the periods in which the transactions occur rather that only in the periods in which cash is received or paid by the enterprise.

____3-4. Actual and/or expected cash inflows during a period from delivering or producing goods, rendering services, or other activities that represent the entity's business purpose.

____3-5. This occurs when goods or services are exchanged for cash or claims to cash; generally, this is when (a) the prices to be received for the products/services become reasonably certain and (b) the prices have been earned by the firm.

____3-6. The process of recording or including the financial measurement of a transaction, event, or circumstance in the firm's measure of current period performance.

___3-7. The outflows or costs of resources during a period used to deliver or produce goods, render services, or carry out other activities that represent the entity's business purpose.

___3-8. The process of including the expenses incurred to produce and sell a product or service in the same time period as the revenues they generated.

___3-9. Resource costs that logically attach to products; product costs are recognized as expenses in the period in which the particular product is sold.

___3-10. Costs that relate more closely to specific time periods than to an identifiable product or service.

___3-11. A firm's increase in wealth over a period of time.

___3-12. Inflows (outflows) of resources from transactions and other events and circumstances which affect the entity during a period but are incidentally related to the entity's business purpose.

___3-13. These are both highly infrequent and unusual.

___3-14. The difference between revenues from operations and related expenses, plus or minus gains or losses, for a given period of time.

___3-15. Income or loss from continuing operations plus or minus extraordinary gains or losses.

A company's accounting records reflected the following information at the end of the year:

Sales for cash	$120,000
Sales on credit	$30,000
Credit accounts not yet collected at year end	$15,000
Received from bank loan	$30,000
Rent paid for this period	$10,000
Office expenses paid for this period	$25,000
Wages paid for work done in preceding period	$2,000
Wages paid for work done this period	$40,000
Total unpaid wages for work done this period	$13,000
Equipment sold (historical cost $10,000, total accumulated depreciation was $6,000)	$3,000

Depreciation recorded for the period	$5,000
Insurance paid for next period	$3,000
Interest paid for this month on bank loan	$300
Uninsured earthquake damage - paid in cash	$7,000
Dividends paid to owners	$4,000

3-16. Total cash receipts from operations were _____

3-17. Total cash disbursements for operations were _____

3-18. Total cash receipts from non-operational activities were
_____.

3-19. Total cash disbursements for non-operational activities
were_____.

3-20. Net cash flow for the period was_____.

3-21. Total revenues for the period were_____.

3-22. Total expenses for the period were_____.

3-23. Operating income for the period was_____.

3-24. Net income for the period was_____.

Determine the effect of each of the following on this period's cash flow. Use the following code.

A = Increases cash flow from operations.
B = Has no effect on cash flow from operations but increases net
cash flow.
C = Decreases cash flow from operations.
D = Has no effect on cash flow from operations but decreases net
cash flow.
E = Has no effect on cash flow.

___3-25. The company pays a supplier for materials received
this month.

___3-26. The company pays a supplier for materials received
last month.

____3-27. The company pays a supplier for materials to be received next month.

____3-28. The company purchases land for $80,000 cash.

____3-29. The company borrows $85,000 from the bank.

____3-30. The company purchases equipment for $50,000 cash.

____3-31. Employees work this month; payday is the first Friday of next month.

____3-32. The company makes cash sales.

____3-33. The company pays owners $15,000 in cash dividends.

____3-34. The company makes credit sales.

____3-35. A customer orders and pays for a product the company will manufacture next period.

____3-36. The company pays the bank $850 interest on the bank loan for this month.

____3-37. The company sells some machinery. The machine had an original cost of $50,000 and has total depreciation of $40,000. The machine is sold for $4,000.

____3-38. The company records depreciation.

____3-39. The company repays the bank $5,000 of the principal on the loan.

____3-40. The company uses supplies on hand.

____3-41. The company buys back stock from one of the owners for $2,000.

____3-42. The company records the use of prepaid insurance.

____3-43. The company receives $200,000 from owner contributions.

____3-44. The company orders $10,000 of raw materials.

___3-45. The company sells some furniture. It had an original cost of $10,000 and total accumulated depreciation of $8,000. It was sold for $5,000.

Determine the effect of each of the following on this period's income. Use the following code.

A = Increases net income from operations.
B = Has no effect on net income from operations but increases net income.
C = Decreases net income from operations.
D = Has no effect on net income from operations but decreases net income.
E = Has no effect on net income.

___3-46. The company pays a supplier for materials received this month.

___3-47. The company pays a supplier for materials received last month.

___3-48. The company pays a supplier for materials to be received next month.

___3-49. The company purchases land for $80,000 cash.

___3-50. The company borrows $85,000 from the bank.

___3-51. The company purchases equipment for $50,000 cash.

___3-52. Employees work this month; payday is the first Friday of next month.

___3-53. The company makes cash sales.

___3-54. The company pays owners $15,000 in cash dividends.

___3-55. The company makes credit sales.

___3-56. A customer orders and pays for a product the company will manufacture next period.

___3-57. The company pays the bank $850 interest on the bank loan for this month.

31

____3-58. The company sells some machinery. The machine had an original cost of $50,000 and has total depreciation of $40,000. The machine is sold for $4,000.

____3-59. The company records depreciation.

____3-60. The company repays the bank $5,000 of the principal on the loan.

____3-61. The company uses supplies on hand.

____3-62. The company buys back stock from one of the owners for $2,000.

____3-63. The company records the use of prepaid insurance.

____3-64. The company receives $200,000 from owner contributions.

____3-65. The company orders $10,000 of raw materials.

____3-66. The company sells some furniture. It had an original cost of $10,000 and total accumulated depreciation of $8,000. It sold for $5,000.

MULTIPLE CHOICE. Select the best response for each of the following, and mark the letter corresponding to your choice.

Questions 67-70

Using the following choices, determine the impact of each transaction on the company's 1988 net operating cash flow, net operating income, and net income.

	1988 net operating cash flow	1988 net operating income	1988 net income
a.	decrease	decrease	decrease
b.	no impact	no impact	no impact
c.	no impact	no impact	decrease
d.	no impact	decrease	decrease
e.	decrease	no impact	no impact

___3-67. The company had an opportunity late in 1988 to purchase a big lot of inventory items for resale at a bargain price. These items were paid for in 1988 and will be sold in 1989.

___3-68. The company borrowed $10,000 (principal amount) on January 1, 1986. The bank charges ten percent interest per year on the borrowed funds. Interest payments will only be made when the company pays the loan back. The principal amount ($10,000) plus all the interest owed will be repaid on December 31, 1990.

___3-69. The company pays a cash dividend of $20,000 to stockholders during 1988.

___3-70. Computer equipment used in the corporate offices was stolen. The theft was unusual, and the company hoped that such theft would not occur again. The stolen computer equipment was not insured.

Questions 71-77

You have the following information about your retail business for its first month of operations:
  i.   You contribute $10,000 of your own money to start the business.
  ii. On the first day of the month you borrow $10,000 from the bank for business purposes. You agree to repay the entire amount plus 12 percent interest at the end of the year.
  iii. During the period sales of $10,000 were recognized. By the end of the period $9,500 had been collected from customers.
  iv. On the last day of the month a customer paid a $100 deposit for goods to be finished and delivered next month.
  v.   During the period, merchandise was purchased for sale for $5,000 in cash. At the end of the period $600 of merchandise was left on hand.
  vi. During the period, employees were paid wages of $2,000 in cash.
  vii. Furniture and fixtures for the store were purchased for $6,000 in cash. You estimate the useful lives of the furniture and fixtures to be five years, with no salvage value.
  viii. Your company is not located in an area that is normally subject to floods. However, during the period a flood caused damage to some of the furniture. The estimated cost of the damage is $1,000. Thus far $800 in repairs have been made, all of which have been paid for in cash.

33

3-71. Total cash receipts from operations are:

    a. $10,000
    b. $10,100
    c. $9,500
    d. $9,600
    e. $20,600

3-72. Total cash disbursements for operations were:

    a. $7,000
    b. $13,000
    c. $7,800
    d. $13,800
    e. none of these

3-73. Total cash receipts from non-operational activities were:

    a. $0
    b. $10,000
    c. $20,000
    d. $20,100
    e. none of these

3-74. Total cash disbursements for non-operational activities were:

    a. $0
    b. $6,000
    c. $6,800
    d. $7,200
    e. none of these

3-75. Total revenues for the month were:

    a. $9,500
    b. $10,100
    c. $19,500
    d. $9,600
    e. $10,000

3-76. Net income from operations for the month was:

    a. $2,500
    b. $2,600
    c. $3,400
    d. $3,500
    e. $3,600

3-77. Net income for the month was:

    a. $2,400.
    b. $2,500.
    c. $2,600.
    d. $3,500.
    e. $3,600.

3-78. The matching principle refers to:

    a. Matching expenses to revenues.
    b. Matching revenues to expenses.
    c. Matching cash outflows to cash inflows.
    d. "a" or "b".
    e. "a" or "c".

3-79. Recording wages earned by employees in the income statement even though the wages will not be paid until a later time is an example of which of the following principles?

    a. Realization principle.
    b. Cost principle.
    c. Matching principle.
    d. Uncertainty principle.
    e. "a" and "c".

3-80. Which of the following help(s) determine when a sale should be included in the income statement?

    a. Realization principle.
    b. Cost principle.
    c. Matching principle.
    d. Uncertainty principle.
    e. "a" and "c".

3-81. Payments of dividends to stockholders.

      a. Increase paid-in capital.
      b. Decrease paid-in capital.
      c. Increase retained earnings.
      d. Decrease retained earnings.
      e. None of the above.

CHAPTER FOUR

BASIC CONCEPTS AND BALANCE SHEET MEASURES

CHAPTER OUTLINE

A. Financial position

1. The balance sheet depicts the financial position of the firm; it indicates

    (a) what resources management has available to operate the business during the year and
    (b) where the money to buy those resources was obtained.

2. The primary elements of the balance sheet are:

    (a) assets,
    (b) liabilities, and
    (c) owners' equity.

3. Assets are

    (a) probable future economic benefits
    (b) embodied in resources that are owned by an entity
    (c) as a result of past transactions or events.

4. "Probable future economic benefits" means the assets will contribute to the firm's profitability.

5. Examples of assets are: cash, accounts receivable, copyrights, patents, land, buildings, and equipment.

6. <u>Liabilities</u> are

   (a) future sacrifices of economic benefits
   (b) which arise from present obligations of the entity to provide assets or services to other parties in the future
   (c) as a result of past transactions or events.

7. Liabilities are one source of money that management can use to purchase assets.

8. Examples of liabilities are: accounts payable, wages and salaries due, mortgages, and notes payable.

9. <u>Owners' equity</u> is interest in the assets of an entity that remains after deducting its liabilities. <u>It is the residual.</u>

10. Owners' equity consists of two elements:

    (a) paid-in capital and
    (b) retained earnings.

11. <u>Paid-in capital</u> represents the owners' contributions to the firm in exchange for ownership interests.

12. <u>Retained earnings</u> equals the cumulative net income of the firm which has not been distributed to owners as dividends.

13. Dividends are distributions of assets made to the firm's owners.

14. Retained earnings does not exist in the form of any specific asset. (It is NOT cash.)

15. Retained earnings does NOT represent a legal claim which the owners have against the entity.

16. Conventionally, the elements of the balance sheet are stated at <u>historical cost</u>.

17. Cost is the amount sacrificed to acquire use of a resource.

18. All assets are recorded at the amount paid for them, regardless of changes in their prices and market values in future periods.

19. Assets acquired through purchase are measured at the amount of cash or other assets given up plus the liabilities incurred.

20. Note carefully that even though assets are defined as "probable future economic benefits", they are NOT measured at the price they will bring when sold. Because the sales price is uncertain, the <u>original cost</u> to the firm is used.

21. The accounting equation is:

ASSETS = LIABILITIES + OWNERS' EQUITY.

22. The equation reflects the fact that the firm has two sources of money to pay for the assets; these are liabilities and owners' equity.

23. The money obtained (from liabilities and owners' equity) equals the cash on hand and that spent for noncash assets.

B. Recognizing events.

1. Two types of events affect the financial status of the firm: external transactions and internal adjustments.

2. <u>External</u> transactions are exchange transactions between the firm and external parties.

3. <u>Internal</u> adjustments are changes in the firm's financial position that are evidenced by observation of events within the entity. These include: cost of goods sold, supplies used, expiration of prepaids, depreciation, and so forth.

4. The financial effects of external transactions and internal adjustments can be analyzed using either the three major elements of the balance sheet or the specific accounts making up each of the major elements.

5. A worksheet can be used to analyze the effects of the transactions and adjustments on a firm. The columns of the worksheet are for specific accounts; the rows are to record the impact of each event on the accounts.

6. Note that the analysis of each event must satisfy the equality condition of the accounting equation. (Each row of the worksheet must balance.)

7. <u>Revenues</u> represent increases in retained earnings.

8. <u>Expenses</u> represent decreases in retained earnings.

9. After analysis of all events affecting the firm during a period, a balance sheet, summarizing the new financial position of the firm, is prepared.

10. The heading of the balance sheet identifies:

    (a) the firm,
    (b) the type of financial statement, and
    (c) the (specific) <u>date</u> at which the financial position was determined.

11. The balance sheet presents lists of all the elements of the firm's financial position (assets, liabilities, and owners' equity) and the amounts at which they have been measured.

12. The heading of the income statement identifies:

    (a) the firm,
    (b) the type of financial statement, and
    (c) the <u>period</u> in the life of the firm (not a specific date) covered by the statement.

13. The income statement presents:

    (a) the revenue recognized during the period,
    (b) the expenses that were matched to that revenue, and
    (c) the resulting income or loss.

14. <u>Net income</u> is the recognized net increase in the ownership interests of the firm that results from its productive activities <u>plus</u> any extraordinary gains or losses.

15. The <u>change</u> between beginning owners' equity and ending owners' equity can be explained by the net income for the period plus additional owner investment and minus any owner withdrawals (dividends).

    Beginning Owners' Equity
    + New owner contributions
    - New owner disinvestments (withdrawals of paid-in capital)
    + Net income
    - <u>Dividends paid</u>
    Ending Owners' Equity

16. Net income measures the increase in assets of all kinds in excess of liabilities.

17. Net income does NOT measure the increase in cash.

18. The income statement does NOT reveal all changes in financial position.

19. The balance sheet shows only the cumulative effects of all events that affected assets, liabilities, and owners' equity. It does not show HOW these changes occurred.

QUESTIONS AND EXERCISES

4-1. Which of the following is NOT considered to be a characteristic or limitation of financial statements as currently prepared?

    a. They provide no projections of future events.
    b. They contain historical, not current values.
    c. They often need narrative explanations to be meaningful.
    d. All of the above are limitations or characteristics of financial statements.

4-2. In preparing the conventional accounting balance sheet at the end of 1988, Claude, the bookkeeper, forgot to adjust the prepaid insurance which expired (was "used up") during the year. The effect of his error on the 1988 balance sheet is:

    a. Assets, no effect; liabilities, no effect; owners' equity, understated.
    b. Assets, overstated; liabilities, no effect; owners' equity, overstated.
    c. Assets, understated; liabilities, no effect; owners' equity overstated.
    d. Assets, understated; liabilities, overstated; owners' equity, overstated.
    e. Assets, understated; liabilities, overstated; owners' equity, overstated.

Use the following information to answer the four questions that follow:

Totals as of:	12/31/89	12/31/90	12/31/91
Assets	$17,000	$45,000	?
Liabilities	2,000	6,000	9,000
Owners' equity	?	?	?

For year ending:	12/31/89	12/31/90	12/31/91
Net income	$7,000	?	$16,000
Dividends	1,000	5,000	2,000
Investments of new capital	?	2,000	1,000

1989 WAS THE **FIRST** YEAR OF OPERATIONS FOR THIS FIRM

4-3. Owners' equity at 12/31/90 was:

   a. $45,000
   b. $15,000
   c. $39,000
   d. $54,000
   e. None of the above.

4-4. Investments of new capital during 1989 were:

   a. $7,000
   b. $9,000
   c. $15,000
   d. $19,000
   e. $21,000

4-5. The net income earned during 1990 was:

   a. $31,000
   b. $17,000
   c. $19,000
   d. $24,000
   e. $27,000.

4-6. The assets at 12/31/91 were:

   a. $63,000
   b. $33,000
   c. $54,000
   d. $45,000
   e. Cannot be determined.

Use the following information on the New Mag Corporation to answer the next six questions.

The New Mag Corporation, a small, two-person magazine/book distributor, began business on January 1, 1991. The company's 1991 transactions are listed below along with some additional information. You may wish to record these transactions and the additional information on a worksheet before answering the questions. Follow conventional accounting principles.

January 2   Stockholders contributed $2,000 cash in exchange for common stock of the New Mag Corporation.

              The company purchased inventory (magazines and books for resale) for $800; they paid $500 in cash and charged the rest.

April 1   Office equipment was purchased for $240 cash. The equipment will be used for five years; no salvage value is expected.

May 1   The company purchased a two-year insurance policy for $120 cash to cover losses on its inventory. The policy is effective from May 1, 1991 to April 30, 1993.

September 15 Inventory originally costing $50 was destroyed in a riot. This was considered an abnormal event and not likely to occur again. Since the destruction was caused by a civil disorder, the insurance company covered only 10% of the loss; it paid $5 cash to New Mag.

November 1   New Mag received its first magazine/book contract with a small medical clinic. New Mag will supply books and magazines to the clinic each month for one year beginning November 1, 1991, with the last delivery in October, 1992. New Mag charges $75 per month for delivering magazines and books to customers. The clinic paid the entire contract in advance: $900 cash.

December 31   The ending inventory has a cost of $730.

All other internal adjustments were made.

ADDITIONAL INFORMATION

	1/1/91	12/31/91
Total Assets	$0	$3,059
Total Liabilities	$0	$1,050
Total Owners' Equity	$0	$2,009

1991 Net Income: $9

4-7.   What was the total amount of insurance expense reported on the company's 1990 conventional accounting income statement?

   a. $0
   b. $5
   c. $40
   d. $120
   e. None of the above.

4-8.   What was the amount of the net ordinary gain (loss) and net extraordinary gain (loss), respectively, reported on New Mag's 1991 conventional accounting income statement?

   a. ($50), $0
   b. $0, ($50)
   c. ($45), $0
   d. $0, ($45)
   e. $0, $0

4-9.   What was the net book value (original cost less accumulated depreciation) of the office equipment on the company's 12/31/91 conventional accounting balance sheet?

   a. $240
   b. $236
   c. $204
   d. $192
   e. None of the above.

4-10. What was the amount of sales revenue reported on New Mag's 1991 conventional accounting income statement?

    a. $5
    b. $150
    c. $155
    d. $900
    e. $905

4-11. What was the New Mag Corporation's 1991 net cash flow (before considering any dividend distributions-if any)?

    a. $1,140
    b. $1,145
    c. $1,745
    d. $1,990
    e. $2,045

4-12. Based on the 12/31/91 ending financial position, did the New Mag Corporation make a 1991 dividend distribution?

    a. Yes, the company did distribute dividends.
    b. No, the company did not distribute dividends.
    c. There is not enough information available to determine whether or not the company distributed dividends.

For the next four questions, use the following:

    a. Decrease in assets, decrease in liabilities.
    b. Decrease in assets, increase in liabilities.
    c. Decrease in assets, decrease in owners' equity.
    d. Decrease in liabilities, increase in owners' equity.
    e. Increase in liabilities, decrease in owners' equity.

Choose the appropriate effect from the list above (a-e) for each of the accounting transactions below.

____4-13. The adjusting transaction to record accrued interest payable.

____4-14. The payment of the interest previously accrued.

____4-15. Repayment of the principal amount of a loan.

____4-16. The adjusting transaction to record accrued wages.

45

4-17. Which of the following is the accounting equation?

   a. Revenues - expenses = Net operating income.
   b. Assets + Liabilities = Owners' equity.
   c. Assets = Liabilities + Owners' equity.
   d. Assets = Liabilities - Owners' equity.
   e. Net Operating Income + (-) Extraordinary gains (losses) = Net income.

4-18. Inventory on January 1, 19X8 was $18,000. During the year, purchases of merchandise totaled $64,000. On December 31, a count of merchandise shows $10,000 is still on hand. What entry would you make to record the count?

   a. Decrease inventory $72,000; decrease retained earnings $72,000.
   b. Increase inventory $10,000; decrease cash $10,000.
   c. Increase inventory $10,000; decrease retained earnings $10,000.
   d. Increase cash $72,000; increase retained earnings $72,000.
   e. None of the above.

4-19. Accrued wages payable is an example of:

   a. Good labor relations.
   b. The realization principle.
   c. The matching principle.
   d. Conservatism.
   e. Poor planning.

4-20. For 1990 Evan's Computers, Inc. reported net income of $130,000 and distributed cash dividends of $50,000 to owners. No additional investments were made by owners. The balance of owners' equity on December 31, 1990, was $190,000. What was the balance of owners' equity on January 1, 1990?

   a. $270,000.
   b. $110,000.
   c. $140,000.
   d. $240,000.

4-21. At the start of the year assets were $80,000 and owners' equity was $20,000. Liabilities increase by $30,000 between the start and the end of the year. Net income for the year was $40,000. Paid-in capital remains unchanged, and there were no dividends. Assets increased (decreased) between the start and the end of the year by:

a. $40,000.
b. $70,000.
c. ($70,000.)
d. $30,000.
e. None of the above.

4-22. Which is an example of an accrued liability?

a. Dividends payable.
b. Accounts payable
c. Bank loan payable.
d. Interest payable.

4-23. If beginning inventory is $1,000, cost of goods sold is $4,000, and ending inventory is $3,000, how much inventory was purchased during the period?

a. $1,000.
b. $2,000.
c. $5,000.
d. $6,000.
e. $7,000.

4-24. Which of the following is an example of an internal adjustment?

a. Payment of one year's rent in advance.
b. Payment of dividends to stockholders.
c. Record monthly depreciation on production equipment.
d. Cash receipt from a customer who is paying for a product which will be delivered next year.
e. None of the above are internal adjustments.

4-25. At the start of the year assets were $110,000 and owners' equity was $30,000. Liabilities decreased by $15,000 between the start and the end of the year. Net income for the year was $45,000. Paid-in capital remained unchanged, and there were no dividends. Assets increased (decreased) between the start and end of the year by:

 a. ($15,000.)
 b. $30,000
 c. $45,000
 d. $95,000
 e. $140,000

4-26. The wages payable account is an example of:

 a. an expense
 b. an asset
 c. a liability
 d. an owners' equity item
 e. a revenue

4-27. A transaction in a company's worksheet has the following entry:

Cash	Machinery	Accumulated depreciation	Retained earnings
4,000	(10,000)	4,500	(1,500)

From this entry, you can tell that:

 a. The entry is incorrect because the accumulated depreciation acccount should have a negative balance.
 b. Machinery with an original cost of $5,500 was sold at a loss of $1,500.
 c. Machinery with an original cost of $4,000 was sold at a loss of $1,500.
 d. Machinery with an original cost of $10,000 was sold for $4,000.
 e. None of the above.

For each transaction described in the following questions, choose the correct option below (a-e) which shows the impact the transaction has on the company's net cash flow, assets, liabilities, paid-in capital, retained earnings, and net income.

	net cash flow	assets	liabilities	paid-in capital	retained earnings	net income
a.	decrease	decrease	no change	decrease	no change	no change
b.	increase	increase	no change	no change	increase	increase
c.	increase	increase	increase	no change	no change	no change
d.	decrease	decrease	no change	no change	decrease	no change
e.	no change	decrease	no change	no change	decrease	decrease
f.	decrease	decrease	decrease	no change	no change	no change
g.	decrease	decrease	no change	no change	decrease	decrease
h.	no change	no change	decrease	no change	increase	increase
i.	no change	no change	increase	no change	decrease	no change

_____4-28. The company records depreciation expense for the year.

_____4-29. The company recognizes the use of one month's rent which was previously paid for (prepaid rent).

_____4-30. The company receives cash from customers who are paying for products which will be delivered next year.

_____4-31. The company pays cash dividends which had been recorded as a liability and a reduction of retained earnings in the previous period.

_____4-32. The company records the declaration of a new dividend.

_____4-33. The company pays wages earned during the period.

_____4-34. The company recognizes revenue from work performed during the period; the customers had already paid for the work in a previous period.

49

CHAPTER FIVE

STATEMENT OF CASH FLOWS

CHAPTER OUTLINE

A. THE NEED FOR CASH FLOW INFORMATION

1. The major purpose of the Statement of Cash Flows (SCF) is to provide information about the firm's cash receipts and cash disbursements during a period of time.

2. Information about current cash flows is useful for predicting future cash flows.

3. The SCF was made mandatory in 1987.

4. The SCF is to be used with related information and disclosures in the Balance Sheet and the Income Statement.

5. The SCF is to help users

   (a) assess the firm's ability to generate positive future net cash inflows,
   (b) assess the firm's ability to meet its obligations, to pay dividends, and to meet its needs for external financing,
   (c) assess the reasons for differences between net income and associated cash receipts and payments, and
   (d) assess the effects on a firm's financial position of both its cash and noncash investing and financing transactions during a period.

6. Requiring a SCF in no way diminishes the importance of the Income Statement as a measure of performance and for predicting the firm's long-run cash-generating ability; both statements are necessary.

7. Excessive reliance on the Income Statement may cause the investor to overlook current shortfalls in the actual flow of cash through the business.

8. The SCF is used for explaining the specific changes that occurred in the balance sheet accounts and their related cash flow effects.

B. CASH FLOWS FROM OPERATING, INVESTING, AND FINANCING ACTIVITIES

1. The objective of the SCF is to explain changes in the cash account according to the management activities that cause the changes; these are: operations, investing, and financing.

2. Operating activities are those transactions and events directly related to the regular production and delivery of goods and services to customers. Basically, these are the CASH EFFECTS of the transactions that impact net income (e.g. cash receipts from sale of goods or services and cash payments for expenses such as inventory, wages, supplies, interest, taxes, etc.).

3. Investment activities include:

   (a) (acquisition) and disposition of assets such as buildings, equipment, land;
   (b) (making) collecting loans (to) from others;
   (c) (purchasing) selling another firm's stock.

   NOTE: the interest earned from making loans to others and the dividends earned from owning the stock of other firms are part of OPERATING activities.

4. Financing activities include:

   (a) obtaining funds from (repaying) repaying creditors;
   (b) selling (repurchasing) the firm's stock;
   (c) the payment of dividends.

   NOTE, however, that the payment of interest on obligations to creditors is an OPERATING activity.

5.   Net cash inflow (outflow) from operations
   +   Net cash inflow (outflow) from investing activities
   ±   <u>Net cash inflow (outflow) from financing activities</u>
       Net cash change for the period

C. PREPARING THE STATEMENT -DIRECT METHOD

1. For the direct method the SCF is prepared using

   a. the beginning-of-the-period and the end-of-the-period balance sheets (to derive the <u>changes</u> for the period).

   b. the Income Statement, and

   c. other relevant information (e.g., items like "there were no equipment sales during the year").

2. Analyzing the accounts and organizing the information.

   a. Determine the <u>change in cash</u> for the period (this is what you want to explain).

   b. **For the OPERATIONS section of the SCF you need to convert each item on the income statement from accrual to cash basis.**

      1. To determine **cash receipts** from operations

         a. begin with the REVENUES from the income statement

         b. and adjust for
            i.   changes in accounts receivable,
            ii.   changes in deferred (unearned) revenue,
            iii. changes in any other related accounts on the balance sheet.

      2. To determine **cash disbursements** for operations

         a. for **EACH EXPENSE** on the income statement examine the balance sheet for related accounts and adjust accordingly

         b. generally, the cost of goods sold expense will need to be adjusted for
            i.   the change in inventories and
            ii.   change in accounts payable.

52

c. for EACH of the other expense items on the income statement, you will have to examine the balance sheet carefully for related accounts.

    i.   For example, if there is a "rent expense" on the income statement, examine the balance sheet for "prepaid rent" and/or "rent payable"; if you find such related items, you will have to use the changes in them to adjust the accrual expense to cash flow for the item.

    ii.   Depreciation expense may be stated separately on the income statement or included with other items such as "operating expenses", "miscellaneous expenses", etc.; as depreciation does NOT require cash, you must adjust the expenses to reflect this.

    iii.   Be very careful, especially if there are "fuzzy" (non-defined) items like "other expenses" on the income statement.

        a. Look for related items on the balance sheet that may apply; items like: prepaid expenses, prepaid taxes, accrued liabilities, taxes payable, wages payable, etc.

        b. All such OPERATIONS related items MUST be used in adjusting from accrual to cash.

3. Now, put together all the information related to operations.

    Cash receipts from operations
- <u>cash disbursements for operations</u>
    net cash inflow (outflow) from operations.

c. For the INVESTING section of the SCF you need to

1. Identify all the accounts on the balance sheet that relate to INVESTING activities (building, equipment, land, patents, loans to others, investment in other firms' stocks, etc.).

2. Analyze the CHANGE in each of the identified accounts.

3. Use these CHANGES in conjunction with the other related information to determine the cash flows from each of the investing items.

   a. **Special attention is required here.**

   b. The sale of long-lived assets normally results in a gain or loss on sale (which is equal to the difference between the proceeds from sale and the book value of the asset). Remember: "book value" is historical cost less accumulated depreciation to date of sale.

   c. This gain or loss is on the income statement.

   d. On the SCF you want only the cash effect of the sale. ANALYZE CAREFULLY.

      i.   For example, assume the data indicate that land was sold for $25,000 cash and that this resulted in a gain of $12,000 because the land had originally cost $13,000.

      ii. The $12,000 gain is on the income statement. Be sure to eliminate its effect when you are doing the operations section of the SCF. You do NOT want it in there because it is not an operations item.

      iii. In the INVESTMENTS section of the SCF you would want to include the $25,000 as a cash inflow.

   4. Now put together all the information related to investments:

      cash inflow from investments
      - cash outflow from investments
      net cash inflow (outflow) from investing activities.

d. **For the FINANCING section of the SCF you need to**

   1. Identify all the accounts on the balance sheet that relate to FINANCING activities (obtaining/ repaying long-term loans, selling/repurchasing the company's own stock, paying dividends).

   2. Analyze the CHANGE in each of the identified accounts.

3. Use these CHANGES in conjunction with the other related information to determine the cash flows from each of the financing items.

    a. Pay special attention to the change in the RETAINED EARNINGS account. You need to check this for dividend payouts.

    b. Remember:

       Beginning retained earnings
      + Net income
      - <u>Dividends</u>
       Ending retained earnings

4. NOTE: some items that do NOT involve CASH must be on the SCF.

    a. For example, if a firm acquires equipment by signing a note payable, this information is included on the SCF as if it were a source (use) of cash. Thus, the purchase of equipment would be treated as a use of cash under INVESTING activities and the note payable would be treated as a source of cash under FINANCING activities.

    b. This is done so that the SCF will provide information about ALL the investing and financing activities of the period, EVEN IF THEY DID NOT INVOLVE CASH.

5. Now put together all the information related to financing:

      cash inflow from financing
    - <u>cash outflow from financing</u>
      net cash inflow (outflow) from financing activities.

3. To prepare the complete SCF, simply present the information you have generated as decribed above so that one can easily see the cash inflows and outflows related to each of the three areas (operations, investing, and financing) and show the net change in cash for the period.

D. PREPARING THE STATEMENT- INDIRECT METHOD (FROM THE APPENDIX TO THE CHAPTER)

1. The difference between the direct and the indirect methods of preparing the SCF is in the way the information for OPERATING ACTIVITIES is obtained. The rest of the procedures are as described above.

2. In preparing the operating activities section of the SCF using the direct method, each of the individual revenue and expense items on the income statement were directly adjusted from an accrual to a cash basis.

3. In preparing the SCF using the INDIRECT method, you begin with net income (rather than the individual revenues and expenses) and make adjustments to remove the noncash revenues and expenses.

4. Again, you use CHANGES in the balance sheet accounts to do the adjusting.

    a. Scan the balance sheets to identify all the accounts related to operations. (Accounts receivable, Inventories, prepaid items, accounts payable, wages payable, interest payable, taxes payable, accrued liabilities, etc.)

    b. Adjust net income by the amount of the CHANGE in the related accounts. Be careful about the direction of the adjustment.

        i.   add decreases in operations-related assets
        ii. subtract increases in operations-related assets
        iii. subtract decreases in operations-related liabilities
        iv. add increases in related operations-liabilities

    c. Add back the amount of the depreciation expense because depreciation does NOT involve cash flows.

        i. Depreciation expense may be identified separately on the income statement.

        ii. If the information is not available on the income statement, you may have to derive depreciation expense as the CHANGE in accumulated depreciation on the balance sheet.

d.   NET INCOME
+ decreases in operations-related assets
- increases in operations-related assets
- decreases in operations-related liabilities
+ increases in operations-related liabilities
+ <u>depreciation expense (and similar non-cash items)</u>
CASH FLOW FROM OPERATIONS

QUESTIONS AND EXERCISES

TRUE-FALSE. Indicate whether each of the following statements is true or false.

_____5-1.   The major purpose of the Statement of Cash Flows is to provide information about the firm's ability to generate net income.

_____5-2.   Information about current cash flows is useful for predicting future cash flows.

_____5-3.   One of the purposes of the Statement of Cash Flows is to help users assess the reasons for differences between net income and associated cash receipts and payments.

_____5-4.   One of the purposes of the Statement of Cash Flows is to help users assess the effects on a firm's financial position of both its cash and noncash investing and financing transactions during a period.

_____5-5.   Excessive reliance on the income statement may cause the investor to overlook current shortfalls in the actual flow of cash through the business.

_____5-6.   One of the purposes of the Statement of Cash Flows is to explain the specific changes that occurred in the balance sheet accounts and their related cash flow effects.

_____5-7. The objective of the SCF is to explain changes in the cash account according to the management activities that cause the changes; these are: <u>operations, investing, and budgeting.</u>

_____5-8. <u>Operating</u> activities are those transactions and events directly related to the regular production and delivery of goods and services to customers.

_____5-9. Cash receipts from sale of goods or services and cash payments for expenses such as inventory, wages, supplies, interest, taxes, etc. appear in the operations section of the statement of cash flows.

____5-10. <u>Investment</u> activities include acquisition and disposition of assets such as buildings, equipment, and land; making/ collecting loans to /from others; and collecting the interest earned from making loans to others.

____5-11. The dividends earned from owning the stock of other firms are part of operating activities on a statement of cash flows.

____5-12. Financing activities include: (a) obtaining funds from and repaying creditors; (b) selling (repurchasing) the firm's stock; and (c) the payment of interest and dividends.

____5-13. The disposition of long-lived assets normally results in a gain or loss on disposal which is equal to the difference between the proceeds from sale and the book value of the asset.

MULTIPLE CHOICE. Select the best response to each of the following, and mark the letter corresponding to your choice.

5-14. If accumulated depreciation increases during the year by $1,000, as a result of this event, the cash flow will:

    a. Increase by $1,000.
    b. Decrease by $1,000.
    c. Remain the same.
    d. None of the above.

5-15. If there is an increase in the Equipment Account of $55,000 during the year, then as a result of this, cash flow from operations will

a. Increase by $55,000.
b. Decrease by $55,000.
c. Remain the same.

5-16. The difference between net cash flow and net operating income is NOT explained by:

a. Long-lived equipment purchased this period.
b. Expenses incurred last period and paid for this period.
c. Revenue realized this period and collected this period.
d. Advances received this period for goods to be delivered next period.
e. Revenue earned this period and collected next period.

5-17. On a statement of cash flows, which item is a use of cash in operations?

a. Repayment of long-term debt.
b. Increase of inventories for sale to customers.
c. Purchase of a depreciable asset.
d. Decrease of accounts receivable.
e. Increase of accounts payable to suppliers.

5-18. A truck was purchased on January 1, 19X5, for $40,000. Its estimated useful life is five years. No salvage value is expected at the end of the five years. On December 31, 19X8, the truck is sold for $5,000 cash. This sale is shown in the statement of cash flows as:

a. A source of $8,000 cash from operations activities.
b. A source of $8,000 cash from investing activities.
c. A source of $5,000 cash from operations activties.
d. A source of $5,000 cash from investing activities.
e. A source of $5,000 cash from financing activities.

5-19. On a statement of cash flows which of the following is NOT a source of cash?

   a. Decrease in accounts receivable.
   b. Sale of additional common stock.
   c. Disposal of long-lived assets above net book values.
   d. Decrease in income taxes payable.
   e. Taking out a new bank loan.

5-20. Which of the following statements is true?

   a. Obtaining funds from owners is classified as an investment activity on a Statement of Cash Flows.
   b. The cash a company paid for interest on bank loans appears as a financing activity on a Statement of Cash Flows.
   c. Cash paid for dividends appears in the operations section of a firm's Statement of Cash Flows.
   d. The cash earned as dividends from owning stocks in other companies appears as part of operations activities.
   e. None of the above is true.

5-21. A worksheet shows an increase in insurance expense of $300 and a corresponding decrease of $300 for prepaid items. If there were no other transactions affecting prepaid items, relative to accrual income, the change in this account:

   a. Increased cash flow for the period.
   b. Decreased cash flow for the period.
   c. Will affect cash flow in later periods.
   d. Had no effect on this period's cash flow.
   e. Should be classified as an investing activity.

5-22. Which of the following items should NOT be classified as a financing activity on a statement of cash flows?

   a. Repurchasing the firm's stock from shareholders.
   b. Repaying the principal on long-term loans.
   c. The dividends earned from owning stocks of other firms.
   d. The interest earned from making loans to other firms.
   e. "c" and "d"

5-23. The beginning balance in accounts receivable was $25,000, cash collections during the period were $165,000, and the ending balance in accounts receivable was $37,500. The revenue from sales during the period was:

  a. $165,000.
  b. $152,500.
  c. $177,500.
  d. $190,000.

5-24. If the beginning balance in prepaid insurance was $375, payments for insurance during the period were $2,100, and ending balance in prepaid insurance was $175, then the insurance expense for the period was:

  a. $2,100
  b. $2,300
  c. $2,475
  d. $2,650

5-25. The wages payable account had a beginning balance of $2,500 and an ending balance of $4,000. Wage expense for the period was $83,000. How much cash was paid for wages during the period?

  a. $85,500
  b. $87,000
  c. $84,500
  d. $81,500

Use the following information from the Belved Company for the next seven questions.

Belved Company
Income Statement
For 19X7

Sales revenue		$480
Cost of goods sold	90	
Wages expense	90	
Advertising expense	30	
Depreciation expense	80	
Rent expense	15	
Interest expense	8	
Total expenses		($313)
Net Income		$167

Belved Company
Balance Sheets

	12/31/X6	12/31/X7
ASSETS		
Cash	$150	$290
Accounts receivable	$100	$200
Inventory	$250	$230
Prepaid rent	$20	$15
Equipment	$600	$700
Accumulated depreciation	($150)	($230)
TOTAL ASSETS	$970	$1,205
LIABILITIES		
Accounts payable	$175	$125
Wages payable	$0	$20
Interest payable	$10	$8
Mortgage payable	$300	$250
OWNERS' EQUITY (OE)		
Paid-in Capital	$485	$685
Retained earnings	$0	$117
TOTAL LIABILITIES AND OE	$970	$1,205

5-26. For 19X7, cash sales and collections were:

    a. $480
    b. $380
    c. $680
    d. $280

5-27. For 19X7, cash paid for inventory was:

    a. $90
    b. $70
    c. $120
    d. $140

5-28. For 19X7, cash paid for wages was:

    a. $90
    b. $110
    c. $70
    d. None of the above.

5-29. For 19X7, cash paid for advertising was:

    a. $30
    b. $80
    c. $25
    d. None of the above.

5-30. For 19X7, cash paid for depreciation was:

    a. $80
    b. $0
    c. $230
    d. None of the above.

5-31. For 19X7, cash paid for rent was:

    a. $15
    b. $30
    c. $20
    d. $10

5-32. For 19X7, cash paid for interest was:

      a. $8
      b. $10
      c. $18
      d. $20

5-33. For 19X7, net cash flow from operating activities was:

      a. $135
      b. $140
      c. $55
      d. $145

5-34. For 19X7, net cash inflow (outflow) from investing activities was:

      a. $100
      b.   ($100.)
      c. $180
      d.   ($180.)

5-35 For 19X7, the net cash inflow (outflow) related to long-term credit activities was:

      a. $250
      b.   ($250.)
      c. $50
      d.   ($50.)

5-36. For 19X7, the net cash inflow (outflow) related to the company's transactions in its own stock was:

      a. $685
      b.   ($685.)
      c. $200
      d.   ($200.)

5-37. For 19X7, the net cash inflow (outflow) from dividend payments was:

      a.   ($117.)
      b.   ($50.)
      c.   ($167.)
      d. None of the above.

5-38. For 19X7, net cash inflow (outflow) from financing activities was:

    a. $100
    b. $200
    c. $300
    d.   ($100.)

5-39. For 19X7, the net increase (decrease) in cash was:

    a. $140.
    b.   ($140.)
    c. $290
    d.   ($290.)

Use the following information for Belved Company for the next seven questions: (INDIRECT METHOD- Statement of Cash Flows.)

Belved Company
Balance Sheets

	12/31/X6	12/31/X7
ASSETS		
Cash	$150	$290
Accounts receivable	$100	$200
Inventory	$250	$230
Prepaid rent	$20	$15
Equipment	$600	$700
Accumulated depreciation	($150)	($230)
TOTAL ASSETS	$970	$1,205
LIABILITIES		
Accounts payable	$175	$125
Wages payable	$0	$20
Interest payable	$10	$8
Mortgage payable	$300	$250
OWNERS' EQUITY (OE)		
Paid-in Capital	$485	$685
Retained earnings	$0	$117
TOTAL LIABILITIES AND OE	$970	$1,205

NET INCOME FOR 19X7 was $167.

5-40. For 19X7, net cash flow from operating activities was:

    a. $135
    b. $140
    c. $55
    d. $145

5-41. For 19X7, net cash inflow (outflow) from investing activities was:

    a. $100
    b.   ($100.)
    c. $180
    d.   ($180.)

5-42. For 19X7, the net cash inflow (outflow) related to long-term credit activities was:

    a. $250
    b.   ($250.)
    c. $50
    d.   ($50.)

5-43. For 19X7, the net cash inflow (outflow) related to the company's transactions in its own stock was:

    a. $685
    b.   ($685.)
    c. $200
    d.   ($200.)

5-44. For 19X7, the net cash inflow (outflow) from dividend payments was:

    a.   ($117.)
    b.   ($50.)
    c.   ($167.)
    d. None of the above.

5-45. For 19X7, net cash inflow (outflow) from financing activities was:

    a. $100
    b. $200
    c. $300
    d.   ($100.)

5-46. For 19X7, the net increase (decrease) in cash was:

 a. $150.
 b.   ($150.)
 c. $290
 d.   ($290.)

CHAPTER SIX

ACCOUNTING FOR THE EFFECTS OF CHANGING PRICES

CHAPTER OUTLINE

1. Changing prices can be caused by technology changes, specific supply and demand changes, or general price trends.

2. Changes in GENERAL PRICE TRENDS (INFLATION) are measured by Price Level Adjusted (PLA) accounting.

3. PLA accounting requires that you

    (a) use price indexes to restate some accounting numbers and
    (b) assess monetary gains and losses.

4. The effects of SPECIFIC PRICE CHANGES are measured by Current Cost (CC) accounting.

5. CC accounting requires that you

    (a) determine the replacement costs of physical assets at the balance sheet date and
    (b) assess the holding gains and losses from owning physical assets during periods of price changes.

CHANGING PRICES AND PRICE INDEXES

1. GENERAL price changes are measured by price indexes. The U.S. Department of Labor publishes the consumer price index for all urban consumers each month.

68

2. The purchasing power of money changes over time.

3. Conventional accounting assumes that the purchasing power of money is constant.

4. Inflation rates (changes in the purchasing power of money) can be measured by comparing the prices of a basket of goods and services at different points in time.

CONSTRUCTING PRICE LEVEL INDEXES

1. Price level indexes state a year's average prices in terms of some other year's (base year) average prices.

2. The index numbers are based on the assumptions

   (a) that relative prices can be accurately determined and
   (b) that the basket of goods and services being measured remains constant.

3. The indexes can be used to create ratios to convert amounts to purchasing power equivalents at different points in time.

   a. Assume that a building was purchased in 19X1 for $100,000 when the price level index was 103.

   b. At the end of 19X4, when the price level index is 115, you wish to prepare financial statements with the amounts measured in terms of "19X4 dollars".

   c. Create a ratio: $\dfrac{\text{price level index at balance sheet date}}{\text{price level index at time of purchase}}$

   d. It may be helpful to think of this as the "**TO / FROM**" ratio:

   $$\frac{\textbf{TO} \quad \text{(the end of period index)}}{\textbf{FROM} \quad \text{(the price level index at time of purchase)}}$$

   e. In this case the ratio is: $\dfrac{115}{103}$

f.   Multiply the historical cost of the item by the ratio.

$$(\$100,000)\frac{115}{103} = \$111,650$$

g.   The cost of the building in terms of the purchasing power of the dollar at the end of 19X4 is $111,650.

PRICE LEVEL ADJUSTED (PLA) FINANCIAL STATEMENTS

1.   These are generally used in areas of high inflation, such as South America. PLA accounting was required in the U.S. from 1979-1985.

2.   Those who support PLA accounting advocate a constant measuring unit.

3.   Those who oppose PLA accounting argue

   (a)   that price indexes are statistical averages which may not be meaningful in individual personal or company situations;
   (b)   that PLA is too costly;
   (c)   that PLA is not very beneficial when the inflation rate is moderate, and
   (d)   that PLA is not well understood by investors.

4.   Since PLA statements apply price indexes to conventional financial statements based on historical costs, they do NOT represent a complete departure from historical cost.

5.   PLA statements are based on a purchasing power concept.

PLA PROCEDURES

1.   Obtain conventional historical-cost-based financial statements.

2.   Select an appropriate price level index to be used (usually that in effect at the end of the accounting period).

3.   Classify all items in the financial statements as MONETARY or NONMONETARY. Monetary items include cash, rights to receive fixed amounts of dollars at future dates and obligations to pay fixed amounts of dollars at future dates.

4. <u>Use the MONETARY items to calculate the monetary gains and losses (purchasing power gains and losses).</u> These gains/losses result from holding monetary items during a period of changing prices.

   a. You can calculate the monetary gain or loss by analyzing each monetary account, one at a time. (See Example 6-4 on page 133 in the text.)

   b. For efficiency, you may calculate the monetary gain or loss by using an estimating procedure. (See Example 6-5 on page 134 in the text.)

5. <u>Restate all NONMONETARY items in the financial statements by applying the appropriate price level index ratio.</u> DO NOT RESTATE THE MONETARY ITEMS.

6. <u>Combine all the information into PLA financial statements.</u>

   a. Your <u>PLA balance sheet</u> will

      i. show the MONETARY ITEMS at their UNadjusted historical cost amounts;
      ii. show the NONMONETARY ITEMS as ADJUSTED by price level ratios.

   b. Your <u>PLA income statement</u> will show:

          Revenues (adjusted by price level ratios)
        - <u>Expenses (adjusted by price level ratios)</u>
          PLA Operating Income
     +/- Extraordinary items (adjusted by price level ratios)
     +/- <u>Monetary gains (losses) *</u>
          PLA Net Income

       * Remember: monetary gains and losses are also called "purchasing power gains and losses".

CURRENT COST (CC) ACCOUNTING

1. Current cost is the normal business cost to obtain currently an existing product or service of equivalent capability.

2. Current cost is a complete departure from historical cost.

3. Current cost is based on a <u>physical capital</u> concept. It views a business enterprise as a reservoir of physical productive capacity used to provide products and services to customers. In order to keep from eroding the physical capital base, the firm must be able to replace these physical resources as needed. Thus, CC involves <u>current</u> replacement cost rather than <u>past</u> transaction cost.

4. The largest impact of CC occurs on nonmonetary assets like inventory, plant and equipment, and land. In CC financial statements these items are stated at their END-OF-PERIOD CC.

5. Holding gains (losses) are calculated as the difference between the CC of an item and its historical cost (HC).

6. Holding gains (losses) are <u>UNrealized</u> if the item has not yet been used or sold by the firm. (e.g., ASSETS such as inventories, plant and equipment).

7. Holding gains (losses) are <u>realized</u> if the item has been sold or consumed (e.g., EXPENSES such as cost of goods sold and depreciation expense).

8.　　　Actual revenues
　- <u>current cost expenses</u>
　　CC OPERATING INCOME

9.　　　CC operating income
　+ realized holding gains
　- <u>realized holding losses</u>
　　CC REALIZED INCOME (= conventional accrual accounting income)

10.　　CC REALIZED INCOME
　+/- <u>CHANGE in unrealized holding gains (losses)</u>
　　CC NET INCOME

11. REMEMBER:
　a. Historical cost accounting tracks nominal financial capital.
　b. PLA accounting tracks the purchasing power of capital.
　c. CC accounting tracks physical capital (productive capacity).

QUESTIONS AND EXERCISES

A. TRUE-FALSE. Indicate whether each of the following statements is true or false.

_____6-1. The use of general price level adjustments in accounting involves measurement of the purchasing power equivalent of original transaction values.

_____6-2. The historical cost principle is abandoned when we use a general price-level adjustment accounting model.

_____6-3. In a period of rising prices, conventional accounting net income is usually a reliable index of disposable wealth.

_____6-4. In periods of static prices the conventional accounting model and the general price-level adjustment model yield identical accounting results.

_____6-5. Price-level adjusted net income usually equals price-level adjusted net operating income.

_____6-6. Monetary assets and liabilities, valued at their nominal (face value) amounts, are always in current dollars.

_____6-7. A monetary gain or loss for a particular monetary asset or liability is determined by subtracting the conventional accounting ending balance from the price-level-adjusted ending balance of the account in question.

_____6-8. If a firm's price-level adjusted net income exceeds its price level adjusted net operating income and if the purchasing power of money increased during the period under consideration, the firm's monetary asset balances must have exceeded its net monetary liability balances during the same period.

_____6-9. If the general price level is changing, the purchasing power of a monetary asset changes in the same direction as the price level change.

_____6-10. Monetary gains and losses measure the financial effects of holding monetary assets and liabilities during a period of change in the general price level.

73

____6-11. Current cost accounting is based on the concept of purchasing power.

____6-12. Current cost accounting does not represent a complete departure from historical cost.

____6-13. Holding gains and losses are computed by using general price indexes.

____6-14. Holding gains and losses are calculated as the difference between the current cost of an item and its historical cost.

____6-15. Current cost operating income plus (minus) realized holding gains (losses) equals realized income; realized income is also equal to conventional historical cost accrual accounting income.

B. MULTIPLE CHOICE. Select the best response to each of the following, and mark the letter corresponding to your choice.

6-16. Monetary gains and losses are characteristic of:

   a. Price-level adjusted accounting.
   b. Current cost accounting.
   c. Cash basis accounting.
   d. Net present value accounting.
   e. Accrual accounting.

6-17. On conventional accounting financial statements, monetary gains and losses are:

   a. Not disclosed.
   b. Shown as extraordinary items.
   c. Considered in arriving at net operating income.
   d. A nonoperating item, but not considered extraordinary.
   e. Not separately reported, but easily calculated from information furnished in cash flow statements.

6-18. During periods of stable price levels, any difference between price-level adjusted net income and price-level adjusted net operating income would be due to:

a. Extraordinary gains or losses.
b. Monetary gains or losses.
c. Holding gains or losses.
d. Speculative gains or losses.
e. None of the above.

6-19. XYZ Company sells games. At December 31, 1993, it has an inventory of 5,000 games costing $10,000. This inventory represents:

a. A current liability.
b. Cost of sales.
c. A nonmonetary asset.
d. A long-lived (fixed) asset.
e. An owners' equity item.

6-20. Supplies on January 1, 19X8 were $18,000. During the year, purchases of supplies totaled $64,000. On December 31, a count of supplies shows $10,000 is still on hand.

Assume both purchases and use of supplies occurred evenly throughout the year. Also, assume the price index moved as follows:

January 1, 19X8	110
Average for 19X8	132
December 31, 19X8	154

What is the monetary gain (loss) from holding supplies during the year?

a. Monetary gain of $5,600.
b. Monetary loss of $5,600.
c. Monetary gain of $4,000.
d. Monetary loss of $4,000.
e. None of the above.

6-21. During inflation, if you are a net creditor you will have a

    a. Monetary gain.
    b. Monetary loss.
    c. No monetary gains or losses.
    d. None of the above.

6-22. On January 1 you had $1,000 in your money market account and owed $2,000 on a tuition loan. On July 1 you received a gift of $2,200 and deposited it in the money market account. During the year, you withdrew a total of $1,980 in equal monthly installments for incidental living expenses. On December 31 you receive $150 interest on your bank deposits. No payments were made during the year on the loan. The price level indexes for the year are as follows:

January 1	100
July 1	110
December 31	120

Your monetary gain or loss for the year was:

    a. $220 loss.
    b. $400 gain.
    c. $180 loss.
    d. $180 gain.
    e. $400 loss.

6-23. Which of the following lists only items that would NOT be adjusted by general price level indexes for changes in the value of the dollar on a price-level adjusted (PLA) balance sheet.

    a. cash, accounts receivable, inventory, machinery.
    b. cash, accounts receivable, machinery.
    c. cash, accounts receivable, inventory.
    d. cash, accounts receivable.
    e. All of the above would be adjusted.

CHAPTER SEVEN

THE FINANCIAL ACCOUNTING INFORMATION SYSTEM

CHAPTER OUTLINE

A. GENERAL LEDGER BOOKKEEPING

1. General ledger bookkeeping uses two interrelated recording devices: the **accounting transaction file (general journal)** and the **general ledger**.

2. An **accounting transaction file (ATF)** is a complete diary of an organization's financial activities. It is maintained in chronological order.

3. Each ATF entry (journal entry) includes: date, the accounts affected, the dollar amounts of the effects, and an explanation of the transaction.

4. Effects of transactions are conventionally recorded in terms of "debits" and "credits"; these terms have no meaning as arithmetic notations.

5. "Debit" is abbreviated "dr"; "credit" is abbreviated "cr".

6. A dr. to an ASSET account indicates an INCREASE.

7. A dr. to a LIABILITY account indicates a DECREASE.

8. A dr. to an OWNERS' EQUITY account indicates a DECREASE.

9. A dr. to an EXPENSE account indicates an INCREASE.

10. A cr. to an ASSET account indicates a DECREASE.

11. A cr. to a LIABILITY account indicates an INCREASE.

12. A cr. to an OWNERS' EQUITY account indicates an INCREASE.

13. A cr. to a REVENUE account indicates an INCREASE.

14. As long as debits equal credits in recording transactions and events in the ATF (general journal), the balance of the accounting equation is maintained.

15. By convention, ATF (journal) entries are prepared with the debit(s) appearing first and to the left; credits are indented to the right and appear after the debits.

16. For example, if a company purchased equipment for $5,000 by paying $1,000 cash and signing a note for the balance, the following ATF (journal) entry would be prepared.

Equipment	$5,000	
Cash		$1,000
Notes payable		$4,000

17. All transactions and events must be recorded in the ATF (journal).

18. Typically, transactions entries are done on a daily basis or in batches throughout the accounting cycle; internal adjustment entries are made at the end of the accounting cycle.

19. The **general ledger file (GLF)** is a collection of all the accounts of the firm.

20. The purpose of the general ledger is to organize the information in the ATF (which is in chronological order) by accounts.

21. Notice that the general ledger does NOT contain any information that has not already been entered in the ATF (journal). The information from the ATF is simply being transferred (posted) to the ledger so that it will be easy to determine the balances in each account. Thus, the information for every transaction/event in the system is recorded twice.

22. A single account from a general ledger is frequently portrayed as a T-account. Again, by convention, debits appear on the left and credits on the right.

23. The balance of any account is the difference between the debit and credit totals.

24. Asset accounts normally have debit balances.

25. Liability and owners' equity accounts normally have credit balances.

26. **TEMPORARY ACCOUNTS** (also called nominal accounts) are used for revenue and expense items.

27. Information regarding revenues and expenses is accumulated in the temporary accounts for a period of time.

28. Temporary revenue and expense accounts make it possible to access easily the information for preparing the period's income statement.

29. At the end of the period, the temporary accounts are closed to the RETAINED EARNINGS account. This accomplishes two things.

> The balances in the temporary accounts are reduced to zero so that the information for the new period will not be mixed in with the information from the period just ended.

> The closing of the temporary accounts to RETAINED EARNINGS (RE) transfers the information regarding NET INCOME to that account so that the relationships beween the balance sheet and the income statement are maintained:

> Beginning RE + Net Income - Dividends = Ending RE

30. For the CLOSING ENTRY all <u>revenue</u> accounts are <u>debited</u> in the amount of their balances and all <u>expense</u> accounts are <u>credited</u> in the amount of their balances; the difference between revenues and expenses (the amount of the net income) is recorded in retained earnings.

    a. If the firm has been profitable, retained earnings will be credited;
    b. If the firm has incurred a net loss, retained earnings will be debited.

31. After all appropriate end-of-period adjusting and closing entries have been recorded in the ATF (journal) and the GLF (ledger), financial statements for the period can be prepared from the balances in the ledger accounts.

32. The statement of financial position (balance sheet) simply collects and organizes all the balances in the permanent asset, liability, and owners' equity accounts.

33. The income statement contains all the temporary account balances which were closed into retained earnings.

34. The statement of cash flows is prepared as described in Chapter Five.

   a. Changes in the account balances are used to determine cash flow effects.
   b. For non-cash accounts, credit changes usually represent sources of cash; debit changes usually represent uses of cash.

35. The set of steps described above is referred to as the accounting cycle. It is summarized as follows.

   a. Systematically collect data associated with transactions.

   b. Record transactions in the ATF (journal) with automatic transfer of the information to the GLF (ledger).

   c. Record end-of-period adjustments in the ATF and the GLF.

   d. Prepare an income statement from the balances of the temporary accounts.

   e. Record closing entry in the ATF and the GLF to transfer the balances of the temporary accounts to retained earnings.

   f. Prepare a statement of financial position (balance sheet) from the balances in the permanent accounts and a statement of cash flow from the balances and changes in the accounts.

36. A **trial balance** is a widely used tool. It is simply a list (in debit and credit format) of the balances in all the accounts (both permanent and temporary) at any point in time.

37. A trial balance is convenient because all of the information is summarized on one or, at most, a few pages.

38. A trial balance may be used for recording interim adjusting entries and avoiding closing entries in preparing financial statements at less than one fiscal year (monthly or quarterly).

THE FINANCIAL ACCOUNTING DATA PROCESSING SYSTEM

1. To have the necessary information firms must create appropriate data bases and data processing systems.

2. Data processing systems consist of:

   - source documents
   - subsidiary journals or registers (sales journal, cash journal, payroll register, etc.)
   - subsidiary ledger accounts
   - standardized procedures

3. A computer system can carry out all necessary data transfer and summarization; however, it does NOT ASSURE PROPER ENTRY OF DATA.

4. Many firms are characterized by several subsystems of the total financial accounting sytem.

5. Accounting subsystems tend to correspond to and are integrated with the operating subsystems of the business.

6. An example of a set of subsystems might include:

   - sales and collections subsystem
   - acquisitions and payments subsystem
   - payroll subsystem
   - inventory /warehousing subsystem
   - capital acquisitions and repayments subsystem

QUESTIONS AND EXERCISES

A. TRUE-FALSE. Indicate whether each of the following statements is true or false.

_____7-1. General ledger bookkeeping uses two interrelated recording devices: the accounting transaction file (general journal) and the general ledger.

_____7-2. Each ATF entry (journal entry) includes: date, the accounts affected, the dollar amounts of the effects, and an explanation of the transaction.

_____7-3. The term "credit" means to increase the balance in the account to which the term is applied.

_____7-4. A debit to an OWNERS' EQUITY account indicates an INCREASE.

_____7-5. A credit to an ASSET account indicates an INCREASE.

_____7-6. A credit to an OWNERS' EQUITY account indicates an INCREASE.

_____7-7. A debit to an ASSET account indicates a DECREASE.

_____7-8. The purpose of the general ledger is to organize the information by accounts.

_____7-9. The balance of any account is the sum of the debit and credit totals.

_____7-10. Liability and owners' equity accounts normally have debit balances.

_____7-11. For the closing entry all revenue accounts are credited in the amount of their balances and all expense accounts are debited in the amount of their balances.

_____7-12. If the firm has incurred a loss for the period, the closing entry will include a credit to retained earnings.

____7-13. Information is entered into the general ledger file before it is entered into the accounting transaction file (general journal).

____7-14. Accounting subsystems tend to correspond to and are integrated with the operating subsystems of the business.

B. MULTIPLE CHOICE. Select the best response to each of the following, and mark the letter corresponding to your choice.

Information for numbers 15-23

Below is the balance sheet for Carsue Company at December 31, 19X4.

Carsue Company
Statement of Financial Position
December 31, 19X4

ASSETS		LIABILITIES AND OWNERS' EQUITY	
Cash	$15,000	Accounts payable	$13,500
Accounts receivable	20,000		
Supplies	5,000		
Equipment	40,000		
Accumulated		Paid-in Capital	35,000
depreciation	(20,000.)	Retained Earnings	11,500
TOTAL	$60,000	TOTAL	$60,000

The following have been recorded in the accounting transaction file (general journal) during 19X5 (dates and explanations have been omitted).

Equipment	$10,000	
Cash		$10,000
Cash	$20,000	
Sales revenue		$20,000
Accounts receivable	$55,000	
Sales revenue		$55,000
Cash	$49,000	
Accounts receivable		$49,000

Supplies	$30,000	
Accounts payable		$30,000
Accounts payable	$25,000	
Cash		$25,000
Wages expense	$17,000	
Cash		$11,000
Wages payable		$6,000
Prepaid rent	$8,000	
Cash		$8,000
Supplies expense	$28,000	
Supplies		$28,000
Rent expense	$3,000	
Prepaid rent		$3,000
Depreciation expense	$7,000	
Accumulated depreciation		$7,000
Cash	$12,000	
Paid-in capital		$12,000
Retained earnings	$5,000	
Cash		$5,000

7-15. Given the preceding information, Carsue's cash account balance is now:

    a. $42,000
    b. $37,000
    c. $25,000
    d. $15,000
    e. None of the above.

7-16. Given the preceding information, Carsue's accounts receivable balance is now:

    a. $20,000
    b. $75,000
    c. $26,000
    d. $124,000.
    e. None of the above.

7-17. Given the preceding information, Carsue's supplies account balance is now:

a. $5,000
b. $35,000
c. $42,000
d. $28,000
e. None of the above.

7-18. Given the preceding information, Carsue's equipment less accumulated depreciation now totals:

a. $50,000
b. $30,000
c. $23,000
d. $13,000
e. None of the above.

7-19. Given the preceding information, Carsue's accounts payable balance is now:

a. $18,500
b. $13,500
c. $43,500
d. $68,500
e. None of the above.

7-20. Given the preceding information, Carsue's Paid-in capital account balance is now:

a. $35,000
b. $12,000
c. $47,000
d. $23,000
e. None of the above.

7-21. Given the preceding information, Carsue's revenues for the period were:

a. $20,000
b. $55,000
c. $75,000
d. $35,000
e. None of the above.

7-22. Given the preceding information, Carsue's expenses for the period were:

a. $55,000
b. $48,000
c. $45,000
d. $17,000
e. None of the above.

7-23. Given the preceding information, the balance in Carsue's prepaid rent account is now:

a. $8,000
b. $3,000
c. $5,000
d. $11,000
e. None of the above.

7-24. Given the preceding information, the balance in Carsue's wages payable account is now:

a. $0
b. $6,000
c. $11,000
d. $23,000
e. None of the above.

7-25. Given the preceding information, Carsue's retained earnings account balance is now:

a. $11,500
b. $31,500
c. $6,500
d. $26,500
e. None of the above.

Information for numbers 26-35.

Mr. Singer buys and sells pianos. The account balances in his books as of January 1, 19X1, were as follows:

Cash	$106,700
Accounts receivable	206,300
Inventory-1,000 pianos at a cost of $500 each	500,000
Equipment	20,000
Accumulated depreciation on equipment	(5,000.)
Accounts payable	92,600
Paid-in capital	15,000
Retained earnings	720,400

The next several items present the data for Mr. Singer's transactions during the year ended December 31, 19X1

Choose the answer that represents the journal entry for each.

7-26.   Singer contributed an additional $50,000 to the firm.

    a. Cash $50,000
           Paid-in capital $50,000

    b. Cash $50,000
           Retained earnings $50,000

    c. Paid-in capital $50,000
           Cash $50,000

    d. None of the above.

7-27.   Singer purchased on credit 200 pianos at a cost of $500 each.

    a. Inventory $100,000
           Sales $100,000

    b. Inventory $100,000
           Accounts payable $100,000

    c. Accounts payable $100,000
           Inventory $100,000

    d. None of the above.

7-28. Singer sold on credit 500 pianos at a price of $800 each.

    a.   Accounts receivable $400,000
           Sales $400,000

    b.   Accounts payable $400,000
           Inventory $400,000

    c.   Accounts receivable $400,000
           Inventory $400,000

    d.   None of the above

7-29. Singer paid his suppliers $115,500.

    a.   Cash $115,500
           Accounts payable $115,500

    b.   Accounts payable $115,500
           Cash $115,500

    c.   Inventory $115,500
           Cash $115,500

    d.   None of the above.

7-30. Singer received from his customers $158,800 on account.

    a.   Accounts receivable $158,800
           Sales $158,800

    b.   Inventory $158,800
           Cash $158,800

    c.   Cash $158,800
           Accounts receivable $158,800

    d.   None of the above.

7-31. <u>Singer incurred and paid other expenses of $48,900.</u>

    a.   Miscellaneous expenses $48,900
           Cash $48,900

    b.   Cash $48,900
           Miscellaneous expenses $48,900

    c.   Supplies $48,900
           Cash $48,900

    d.   None of the above.

7-32. <u>Singer purchased additional equipment for $15,000.</u>

    a.   Cash $15,000
           Equipment $15,000

    b.   Equipment $15,000
           Cash $15,000

    c.   Equipment $15,000
           Retained earnings $15,000

    d.   None of the above.

7-33. <u>Singer recorded depreciation of $3,500 on equipment.</u>

    a.   Depreciation expense $3,500
           Accumulated depreciation $3,500

    b.   Depreciation expense $3,500
           Depreciation payable $3,500

    c.   Accumulated depreciation $3,500
           Depreciation expense $3,500

    d.   None of the above.

7-34. <u>Singer counted the inventory; 700 pianos remain.</u>

    a. Inventory   350,000
           Cost of goods sold   350,000

    b. Cost of goods sold   350,000
           Inventory   350,000

    c. Cost of goods sold   250,000
           Inventory   250,000

    d. Inventory   250,000
           Cost of goods sold   250,000

7-35. Given the information in questions 26-34, what was Mr. Singer's net income for the period?

    a. $400,000
    b. $150,000
    c. $101,100
    d. $97,600
    e. None of the above.

CHAPTER EIGHT

REVENUE RECOGNITION AND MEASUREMENT ISSUES

CHAPTER OUTLINE

I. REVENUE RECOGNITION- When is the revenue earned?

1. Questions arise when:
   a. the time period for the earning process is long and/or
   b. the ultimate collection of the sales price is uncertain.

2. Generally, revenue is realized (earned) when:
   a. the price to be received is reasonably certain <u>and</u>
   b. the firm does not face any substantial production steps.

A. Receipt of Order

1. This does not justify recognition of revenue, as the firm has not produced/delivered the products.

2. If advance payment is received with the order, it represents a <u>liability</u> until the order is filled.

B. Point of Production

1. The firm has produced something but has not yet made a sale.

2. Normally, no revenue is recognized until a sale is made.

3. In certain restricted cases where there is an effective government-controlled market at a fixed monetary value, revenue may be recognized at point of production (gold, silver, certain agricultural products, etc.).

C. Long-Term Contracts

1. Percentage-of-completion method

a. A portion of the estimated profit is assigned to each period in which the firm works on the project.

b. The portion of the work completed during the period can be estimated by

    i. the ratio of costs incurred by the end of the period to the estimated total cost of the completed project or

    ii. an independent expert's appraisal of the physical percentage of completion.

c. This method reflects the productive activities of the firm, but it introduces a degree of uncertainty in measuring income as it is based on estimates.

d. This method should be used when the estimates can be made with an acceptable degree of accuracy.

2. Completed contract method

a. No revenue is recognized until completion.

b. All costs are accumulated in a construction-in-process account until delivery.

c. At delivery
    i. the total sales price is recognized as revenue;
    ii. the costs accumulated are recognized as expense;

d. Accomplishment is associated only with the final period.

e. Any payments received from the customer during the construction process are recorded as a liability until completion of the project.

f. This method avoids dealing with the estimates necessary in percentage-of-completion, but it does not reflect the productive activities of the firm over time.

D. Value Accretion, Appreciation and Discovery

1. Revenue should NOT be recognized on the basis of accretion, appreciation or discovery.

2. The prices in any such value enhancements are typically not certain enough to warrant their recognition.

E. Credit Sales

1. Estimating bad debts

a. The matching principle requires that bad debt expense be recognized in the period in which the sale giving rise to the account is recognized as revenue.

b. The amount of the expense is estimated from the firm's historical experience with accounts.

c. The amount may be determined in a number of different ways, as long as the technique is
    i. systematic,
    ii. related to actual bad debts experience, and
    iii. consistent from period to period.

Bad debt expense
    Allowance for doubtful accounts
To record estimated bad debts related to the period's sales.

d. The "Allowance for doubtful accounts" is contra to accounts receivable and appears on the statement of financial position (balance sheet).

e. The actual write-off has NO EFFECT on EITHER the income statement OR the net realizable value of accounts receivable on the balance sheet.

Allowance for doubtful accounts   XX
    Accounts receivable   XX
To record the write-off of an individual account receivable

2. Installment sales method

a. This method is used in those cases in which the uncertainty regarding ultimate collection of cash is so great that using an allowance for doubtful accounts is insufficient, but the uncertainty is not so extreme that the cost recovery method would be required.

b. The profit to be recognized in any period is determined by multiplying the total potential profit by the ratio of cash collections in that period to the total cash collections to be made from the sale.

(Potential profit) $\dfrac{\text{Cash collections during the period}}{\text{Total cash collections to be made}}$

c. The entry to record the sale is:

Cash
Installment contracts receivable
    Inventory
        Deferred income-installment contracts
        Realized income-installment contracts
To record installment sales.

d. Subsequently, as each cash payment is received:

Cash
    Installment contracts receivable
To record receipt of payment on installment contracts.

Deferred income-installment contracts
    Realized income-installment contracts
To record realized income on installment contracts.

3. **Cost recovery method**

a. When the degree of uncertainty regarding ultimate collection of cash is extreme, the cost recovery method may be warrranted.

b. This very conservative method defers recognition of all income until the cost of the product sold has been <u>fully recovered</u>.

c. After the total cost of the product has been recovered, all subsequent cash collections would be recognized as profit.

d. This method is rarely used.

II. REVENUE MEASUREMENT (How much has been earned?)

A. Goods and Future Services

1. The sales price may include goods that are delivered at the date of sale <u>and</u> the promise to provide future services.

2. Do not recognize the total sales price as revenue of the current period when the company has not earned the revenue related to the future services.

3. Allocation is necessary.

   a. **Financing services**

      i. If the period of time between the date of sale and the collection of cash is substantial, recognition should be given to the <u>opportunity cost</u> incurred by the seller in waiting to collect the cash.

      ii. The difference between the total price which will eventually be collected and the cash equivalent (present value) of the future payments at the point of sale is the price paid for the financing services.

      iii. Financing revenue should be recognized as earned over the collection period of the receivable.

   b. **Warranty services**

      i. When merchandise is sold with a guarantee, the selling price is composed of two elements: product and warranty.

      ii. The price for the product is earned at sale.

      iii. The price of the warranty is earned over the life of the guarantee.

   c. **Franchising services**

      i. The franchisor typically receives relatively large initial payments but delivers relatively little product when the franchising operation begins.

      ii. Revenue should be recognized only as earned.

B. Discounts, Returns and Allowances

1. Price discounts

a. These discounts are means of adjusting the set of list prices to prevailing or competitive prices.

b. Do NOT base revenue on the list price.

2. Cash discounts

a. These are granted for prompt payment.

b. The seller can record revenue at the gross amount and then deduct the cash discount as an offset against revenue or as a cash discounts expense.

c. Alternatively, the seller can record revenue net of the discount. If the customer fails to take the discount, the seller records additional income from the discount allowed but not taken.

3. Merchandise returns

a. Generally, if firms allow customers to return merchandise, the returns are accounted for separately.

Sales returns
    Accounts receivable (or cash)

Merchandise inventory
    Cost of merchandise sold

b. The "sales returns" is deducted from the total in the sales revenue account, leaving the net sales figure in the income statement.

4. Sales allowances

a. Allowances usually result from defective merchandise.

b. Allowances are reductions in revenue and the customers' payments.

Sales allowances
    Accounts receivable (or cash)

c. The balance in "sales allowances" is a deduction from the sales revenue.

d. No adjustment to the inventory account is made.

QUESTIONS AND EXERCISES

A. TRUE-FALSE. Indicate whether each of the following statements is true or false.

_____8-1. If the time period for the earning process is short, questions arise as to the period in which the revenue should be recognized.

_____8-2. Generally, revenue is realized (earned) when both the price to be received is reasonably certain and the firm does not face any substantial additional production steps.

_____8-3. In general, firms should recognize revenue at the completion of the production process.

_____8-4. Under the percentage-of-completion accounting method a portion of the estimated profit is assigned to each period in which the firm works on a long-term project.

_____8-5. Under the percentage-of-completion method of accounting, the portion of the work completed during the period can be estimated by an independent expert's appraisal of the physical percentage of completion.

_____8-6. The percentage-of-completion method reflects the productive activities of the firm, but it introduces a degree of uncertainty in measuring income.

_____8-7. Under the completed contract method of accounting for long-term projects no revenue is recognized until completion.

_____8-8. Under the completed contract method of accounting for long-term projects the total sales price is recognized as revenue and all the costs accumulated are recognized as expense at delivery.

_____8-9. Given that the price of oil has recently increased substantially due to political events, oil companies may recognize revenue based on the appreciation.

_____8-10. Since it is impossible to know which customers will fail to pay their bills, companies that make credit sales are not required to account for bad debts until they are actually written off.

_____8-11. The matching principle requires that bad debt expense be recognized in the period in which the sale giving rise to the account is recognized as revenue.

_____8-12. A company may determine the amount of their bad debt expense in a number of different ways, as long as the technique is (1) systematic, (2) related to actual bad debts experience, and (3) consistent from period to period.

_____8-13. To record estimated bad debts related to the period's sales a firm would debit "bad debt expense" and credit "allowance for doubtful accounts".

_____8-14. The "Allowance for doubtful accounts" appears on the income statement.

_____8-15. For companies that match bad debt expense to the revenue associated with the expense, the actual write-off of an account receivable reduces net income for the period in which the write-off occurs.

_____8-16. If collection of a credit sale is highly uncertain, revenue may be recognized using the cost recovery method.

_____8-17. Under the installment sales method, the profit to be recognized in any period is determined by multiplying the total potential profit by the ratio of cash collections in that period to the total cash collections to be made from the sale.

____8-18. Under the installment sales method of revenue recognition some profit is recognized each time cash is received.

____8-19. When the degree of uncertainty regarding ultimate collection of cash is extreme, the cost recovery method may be warrranted.

____8-20. The cost recovery method of revenue recognition is more frequently used than the installment sales method.

____8-21. If the period of time between the date of sale and the collection of cash is substantial, recognition should be given to the opportunity cost incurred by the seller in waiting to collect the cash.

____8-22. Financing revenue should be recognized as earned over the collection period of the receivable.

____8-23. At the point when merchandise is sold with a guarantee, the company should record only revenue related to the price of the product.

____8-24. Price discounts are a means of adjusting the set of list prices to prevailing or competitive prices.

____8-25. Cash discounts are granted for prompt payment.

____8-26. If cash discounts are granted, the seller may record either revenue at the gross amount or revenue net of the discount.

____8-27. Generally, if firms allow customers to return merchandise, the returns are accounted for separately.

8-28. The Scree Company made $105,000 in credit sales during their first year in business. They collected $80,000 from their credit customers and estimated that bad debts would be 3% of their credit sales for the period. They also wrote off accounts that totaled $2,000 during the period. The balance in the accounts receivable account at the end of the period (after all appropriate adjusting entries) is:

 a. $25,000.
 b. $23,000.
 c. $21,850.
 d. $19,850.
 e. None of the above

8-29. The Scree Company made $105,000 in credit sales during their first year in business. They collected $80,000 from their credit customers and estimated that bad debts would be 3% of their credit sales for the period. They also wrote off accounts that totaled $2,000 during the period. The net realizable value of accounts receivable at the end of the period (after all appropriate adjusting entries) is:

 a. $25,000.
 b. $23,000.
 c. $21,850.
 d. $19,850.
 e. None of the above

8-30. The Scree Company made $105,000 in credit sales during their first year in business. They collected $80,000 from their credit customers and estimated that bad debts would be 3% of their credit sales for the period. They also wrote off accounts that totaled $2,000 during the period. Bad debt expense for the period was:

 a. $2,000.
 b. $3,150.
 c. $5,150.
 d. $1,150.
 e. None of the above.

8-31. The Scree Company made $105,000 in credit sales during
their first year in business. They collected $80,000 from
their credit customers and estimated that bad debts would
be 3% of their credit sales for the period. They also wrote
off accounts that totaled $2,000 during the period. The
balance in the "allowance for doubtful accounts" account at
the end of the period (after all appropriate adjustments
have been made) is:

a. $2,000.
b. $3,150.
c. $5,150.
d. $1,150.
e. None of the above.

8-32. In 1990 the Tonker Construction Company signed a
contract to build a project for $28 million. The company
estimates that its costs will total $21 million and that it
will take three years to complete construction.   During
the first year of construction Tonker incurred $6 million in
costs. By the end of the second year Tonker had accumulated
a total of $18 million in construction costs; the company
continues to believe that total costs will be $21 million.
Using the percentage-of-completion method, how much
profit should Tonker recognize for the second year of work
on the project?

a. $16 million.
b. $24 million.
c. $ 6 million.
d. $ 4 million.
e. None of the above.

8-33. The Wim Company signed a contract to build a community center. Total revenue is $32 million, total costs are estimated to be $26 million, and the project is expected to take three years to complete. The company has justifiably decided to use the completed-contract method of accounting. During the first year the company incurred costs of $14 million, and during the second year an additional $6 million in costs was incurred. The financial statements at the end of year two would include:

a. Contract in Process, $26 million.
b. Contract in Process, $20 million.
c. Contract in Process, $14 million.
d. Contract in Process, $ 6 million.
e. None of the above.

8-34. Slick Sales Company sold a product which had cost them $5,000 for $10,000. They received a down payment of $2,000 and additional payments of $4,000 during the accounting period. The company justifiably decided to account for the transaction using the installment sales method. The amount of income realized during the period was:

a. $3,000.
b. $4,000.
c. $5,000.
d. $6,000.
e. None of the above.

8-35. The Justin Company sold a product which had cost $10,000 for $15,000. Justin justifiably decided to account for the sale using the cost recovery method. The company received a $7,000 down payment and an additional $4,000 in cash payments during the year. Realized income for the year from this sale was:

a. $15,000.
b. $11,000.
c. $ 5,000.
d. $ 1,000.
e. None of the above.

8-36. The Wheel 'N Deal Company sold a product to a customer on December 31. The buyer agreed to pay $1,000 as a down payment and to pay $1,000 per year at the end of each of the next four years. The present value of the total cash flows was $4,169. In the year of the sale, Wheel 'N Deal should record:

a. Sales revenue of $5,000.
b. Sales revenue of $1,000 and Financing revenue of $4,000.
c. Sales revenue of $4,169 and Financing revenue of $831.
d. Sales revenue of $4,169.
e. None of the above.

8-37. The Wheel 'N Deal Company sold a product to a customer on December 31, 1990. The buyer agreed to pay $1,000 as a down payment and to pay $1,000 per year at the end of each of the next four years. Given the ten percent interest rate, the present value of the total cash flows was $4,169. For the year 1991, Wheel 'N Deal should record:

a. Financing revenue of $1,000.
b. Financing revenue of $ 317.
c. Financing revenue of $ 400.
d. Financing revenue of $208.
e. None of the above.

8-38. On December 31, 1990, Mega Company sold a sewing machine for $495. The sale included a warranty covering parts and labor for one year. Mega believes that it would be appropriate to sell the machine without the warranty for $345 and that the average cost of servicing defective sewing machines is $125. In the year of the sale Mega should record:

a. Sales revenue of $495.
b. Sales revenue of $345 and warranty revenue of $150.
c. Sales revenue of $345 and warranty revenue of $25.
d. Sales revenue of $345 and a liability of $125.
e. None of the above.

CHAPTER NINE

ASSET MEASUREMENT AND EXPENSE RECOGNITION

CHAPTER OUTLINE

ASSET MEASUREMENT

1. According to the cost principle assets, liabilities, and owners' equity are recognized at their historical cost.

2. Establishing historical cost is relatively easy when cash is paid. However, if some noncash resources are exchanged, determining historical cost is more problematic.

3. In general, one measures the cost of an asset by applying one of the following criteria, in order of priority:

   a. Cash or other monetary consideration paid.

   b. Cash or other monetary consideration paid, plus the current market value of any nonmonetary consideration given.

   c. Current market value of monetary and nonmonetary consideration received.

   d. Cash or other monetary consideration paid, plus the unexpired cost of nonmonetary consideration given.

4. Choice of the appropriate criterion depends upon the order of priority of the asset measurement criteria and the relative reliability of the estimated current market values.

5. In addition to its purchase price, the cost of an asset includes

all outlays to acquire, transport, transform, and install the asset.

6. However, costs (if any) related to the removal of old assets are incorporated into the calculation of the gain or loss on the old asset.

EXPENSE RECOGNITION

1. There is a measurement linkage between the statement of financial position and the income statement.

2. The amount assigned to the ending balance of an asset or liability is a determinant of the related expense measure; if the expense is measured independently, the expense is a determinant of the ending balance in the asset or liability account.

3. The fundamental problem is to determine <u>how to allocate the costs of resources between expense of the period and asset amount at the end of the period.</u>

   a. One can determine the costs of resources used during the period to generate revenue. Those costs then become expenses for the period and the remaining costs are the balance in the asset account at the end of the period.

   b. Alternatively, the asset can be valued at the end of the period as to its future service potential, or ability to generate additional revenue. The expense then is the change in asset value from the beginning to the end of the period.

INVENTORY

1. Physical quantities

   a. The first problem is determining the physical quantities on hand at the end of the period and the physical quantities sold during the period.

   b. Generally, units on hand at the end of a period are determined by a physical count; one then infers the number of units sold during the period from this count and the records of what units were available. For example, if a firm has 200 units of inventory on hand at the beginning of the period and purchases 800 during the period, there were 1,000 units available for sale during the period. If the count at the end of the period shows 100 units remaining in inventory, one concludes that 900 units were sold during the period.

2. Assignment of cost

   a. Specific identification. This method tracks the costs of each specific item in inventory; when that item is sold, its costs are assigned to cost of goods sold for the period. This method is feasible only when the inventory items are uniquely identifiable or of sufficient market value to justify it.

   b. Average cost method. For this method the total cost of the inventory available is divided by the number of units available to determine an average cost per unit. Cost of goods sold is calculated by multiplying the number of units sold by the average cost per unit. The amount assigned to ending inventory is the number of units remaining multiplied by the average cost per unit.

   c. First-in, First-out (FIFO) method. FIFO assumes that the earliest inventory items purchased are the first items sold. The unit costs of the earlier purchases are assigned to cost of goods sold; the unit costs of the later purchases are assigned to ending inventory.

   d. Last-in, First-out (LIFO). Under the LIFO method, it is assumed that the items sold were the items which the firm had acquired most recently.

   e. Only the specific identification method results in an exact matching of costs with the revenue generated by specific items.

   f. During periods of changing prices for the inventories both the balance sheet and the income statement are affected by the accounting method chosen. Thus, even though the same number of physical units are actually bought and sold, "the facts" are reported differently according to the costing method chosen.

   g. When prices are rising, FIFO will produce a higher income number and a lower ending inventory balance than LIFO.

i.   This is because FIFO assumes that the units sold were the first ones in and, thus, those with the lower unit costs.

ii. This results in a cost of goods sold figure based on the earlier lower costs; a lower expense results in a higher income.

iii. The ending inventory under FIFO is composed of those units purchased most recently and at a higher cost; thus, the ending inventory balance would be higher under FIFO than under LIFO.

3. Departure from cost basis

   a. Lower-of-Cost-or-Market-Rule

      i.   Inventory is initially recorded at historical cost, and the ending inventory balance is calculated using one of the methods described previously.

      ii. The cost-based ending inventory balance is then compared with the current replacement cost or market value of the inventory.

      iii. The ending inventory must be presented at lower of cost or market.

           If market value exceeds cost, the inventory is presented at cost.

           If cost exceeds market value, the balance in ending inventory must be reduced to market value, and a loss is recorded.

   b. Obsolete or damaged merchandise. The costs of these items must be decreased or removed from the inventory so that the amount shown for inventory represents no more than the amount for which the inventory can be sold.

4. Manufacturing costs.

   a. Manufacturing firms generally have three categories of inventories: raw materials, work-in-process, and finished goods.

b.   Beginning raw materials
+ purchases of raw materials
- raw materials used in production
  ending raw materials inventory.

c.   Beginning work-in-process
+ raw materials used
+ the cost of labor employed in production
+ appropriate overhead
- the cost of units completed during the period and
   transferred to finished goods
  ending work-in-process.

d.   Beginning finished goods
+ goods completed and transferred in during the period
- goods sold during the period
  ending finished goods.

5. Periodic and perpetual basis

  a. Under a periodic inventory method the allocation between
      cost of goods sold and ending inventory is made at the end
      of the accounting period; the physical count of ending
      inventory units is used to determine the allocation.

  b. Under a perpetual inventory method the cost of goods sold
      is assessed throughout the period as sales are made.

  c. If purchases and sales are intermingled throughout the
      period, the periodic and perpetual methods will produce
      different figures for cost of goods sold and ending
      inventory for the LIFO and Average Cost methods.

LONG-LIVED ASSETS

1. The chief difference between inventories and long-lived
    assets is that long-lived assets are acquired for USE rather
    than for sale.

2. In addition, the benefits to be derived from the long-lived
    assets generally extend over a much longer period of time.

3. Tangible assets include such items as: buildings, machinery, vehicles, and natural resources like land and mineral rights.

4. Intangible assets include such items as: patents, copyrights, franchises, and trademarks.

5. Maintenance and Improvements

   a. If expenditures are made to maintain an asset's operating efficiency, they are regarded as normal repairs and maintenance and reported as <u>expenses</u> in the period in which the expenditures are made.

   b. If expenditures are made to increase the level of benefits to be derived from the asset, they are added to the unexpired cost of the asset and then matched against revenue in future periods.

6. Depreciation expense

   a. One approach to matching the cost of the asset with the revenue it generates is based on the <u>output of the asset</u>. This method is preferable when we can determine fairly accurately an identifiable output from the asset.

   b. A second approach to measuring current period expense is based on the <u>passage of time</u>. This requires the identification of three elements: the useful life of the asset, the market value of the asset at the end of its useful life (salvage or residual value), and a method of depreciation.

      i. <u>Straight-line</u> depreciation allocates an equal portion of the depreciable cost (cost less salvage value) of the asset to each time period during its useful life.

      ii. <u>Sum-of-the-years'-digits</u> method of depreciation produces larger measures of expense in the early years of the life of an asset by applying decreasing depreciation rates to the depreciable cost.

          The depreciation rate is a fraction.

          The numerator is the number of years of useful life remaining for the asset at the beginning of the period.

The denominator is the sum of the digits from 1 to n where n is is the number of years of useful life that the asset is expected to be productive.

The fraction is multiplied by the depreciable cost (cost less salvage value) of the asset.

   iii. <u>Declining balance method</u> depreciation also produces higher depreciation expense in the early years of an asset's life.

The declining balance method requires that a fixed percentage be applied to the book value (NOT depreciable cost) of the asset as of the beginning of each period to determine the expense for the period.

Frequently, the percentage is 150% or 200% of the straight-line rate.

  c. The different methods of calculating depreciation expense result in different net incomes and asset values on the balance sheet in each year of the asset's life.

  d. In selecting a depreciation method the accountant may consider the pattern of related costs such as repairs and maintenance or the expected revenue patterns.

7. Land and Natural Resources

  a. The allocation of the cost of natural resources to time periods is referred to as <u>depletion expense</u> (rather than depreciation expense).

  b. In many cases the production or output method of recognizing the expense is used.

  c. The cost of land owned for use as a site for a company's manufacturing, marketing, or administrative operations is NOT allocated over time.

  d. However, land held for the natural resources it contains is accounted for at cost less accumulated depletion.

8. Intangible Assets

  a. Intangible assets lack physical substance.

b. The cost incurred to acquire an intangible asset is allocated over its useful life.

c. Patents have a legal life of 17 years.

d. The allocation of the cost of an intangible is referred to as "<u>amortization</u>" rather than "depreciation" or "depletion".

e. No accumulated amortization account is used; rather, the amortization expense is a direct reduction to the original cost of the asset.

9. Disposal of Long-lived Assets

a. When assets are sold, if there is a difference between the book value (cost less accumulated depreciation) and the sales proceeds, the difference is treated as a gain or loss.

b. If there are additional expenses incurred to dispose of the asset, these expenses are deducted from the proceeds in determining the gain or loss.

c. Such gains and losses are components of income from continuing operations.

d. According to one method, when an asset is traded in to acquire a new asset of the same kind,

   i.   the gain or loss is the difference between the book value of the old asset and its market value;
   ii. the new asset is recorded as the total of any cash paid plus the market value of the traded-in asset.

e. Under an alternative method, when an asset is traded in to acquire a new asset of the same kind,

   i.   the new asset could be recorded as the sum of the cash payment plus the unexpired cost of the traded-in asset;
   ii. this results in no gain or loss being recognized on the disposition of the old asset.

A. TRUE-FALSE. Indicate whether each of the following statements is true or false.

_____9-1.   In general, assets, liabilities, and owners' equity are recognized at their historical cost.

_____9-2.   In establishng the cost of an asset priority would be given to the value of cash or other monetary consideration paid plus the current market value of any nonmonetary consideration given rather than to the current market value of monetary and nonmonetary consideration received.

_____9-3.   In choosing among the criteria for establishing the cost of an asset the accountant should evaluate the relative reliability of the estimated current market value.

_____9-4.   In addition to its purchase price, the cost of an asset includes all outlays to acquire, transport, transform, and install it.

_____9-5.   Costs (if any) related to the removal of old assets are incorporated into the calculation of the gain or loss on the old asset.

_____9-6.   The amount assigned to the ending balance of an asset or liability is a determinant of the related expense measure.

_____9-7.   The amount assigned to the ending balance of an asset or liability is not necessarily influenced by the related expense account.

_____9-8.   The method by which depreciation expense is determined does not necessarily affect the ending balance in the related asset account.

_____9-9.   If one knows the number of inventory units on hand at the end of a period and the number of units available for a period, one can infer the number of units sold during the period.

116

_____9-10. When using the First-in, First-out method of inventory costing, the unit costs of the earlier purchases are assigned to cost of goods sold; the unit costs of the later purchases are assigned to ending inventory.

_____9-11. Of all the inventory costing methods, only the specific identification method results in an exact matching of costs with the revenue generated by specific items.

_____9-12. Different inventory costing methods result in different amounts being reported in the financial statements because different numbers of physical units are actually bought and sold.

_____9-13. When prices are rising, FIFO will produce a higher income number and a lower ending inventory balance than LIFO.

_____9-14. When prices are rising, LIFO will produce a higher income number and a lower ending inventory balance than FIFO.

_____9-15. The ending inventory must be presented at the lower of cost or market.

_____9-16. If cost exceeds market value, the ending inventory is presented at cost.

_____9-17. If market value exceeds cost, the balance in ending inventory must be presented at cost.

_____9-18. Manufacturing firms generally have three categories of inventories: raw materials, work-in-process, and finished goods.

_____9-19. Beginning raw materials less purchases of raw materials plus raw materials used in production yields the ending raw materials inventory.

_____9-20. Beginning work-in-process plus raw materials used plus the cost of labor employed in production less appropriate overhead less the cost of units completed during the period and transferred to finished goods yields ending work-in-process.

_____9-21. Under a periodic inventory method the allocation between cost of goods sold and ending inventory is made at the end of the accounting period; the physical count of ending inventory units is used to determine the allocation.

_____9-22. Under a perpetual inventory method the cost of goods sold is assessed throughout the period as sales are made.

_____9-23. If purchases and sales are intermingled throughout the period, the periodic and perpetual methods will produce different figures for cost of goods sold and ending inventory for the LIFO and Average Cost methods.

_____9-24. Tangible assets include such items as: patents, copyrights, franchises, and trademarks.

_____9-25. If expenditures are made to maintain an asset's operating efficiency, they are regarded as normal repairs and maintenance and reported as <u>expenses</u> in the period in which the expenditures are made.

_____9-26. If expenditures are made to increase the level of benefits to be derived from an asset, they are added to the unexpired cost of the asset and then matched against revenue (depreciated) in future periods.

_____9-27. One approach to matching the cost of the asset with the revenue it generates is based on the output of the asset.

_____9-28. The sum-of-the-years'-digits method of depreciation produces larger measures of expense in the early years of the life of an asset by applying decreasing depreciation rates to the depreciable cost.

_____9-29. The declining balance method requires that a fixed percentage be applied to the depreciable cost of the asset as of the beginning of each period to determine the expense for the period.

_____9-30. The different methods of calculating depreciation expense result in different net incomes on the income statement and asset values on the balance sheet in each year of the asset's life.

____9-31. The cost of land owned for use as a site for a company's manufacturing, marketing, or administrative operations is allocated over time.

____9-32. Patents have a legal life of 27 years.

____9-33. The allocation of the cost of an intangible is referred to as "amortization" rather than "depreciation" or "depletion".

____9-34. When assets are sold, if there is a difference between the book value (cost less accumulated depreciation) and the sales proceeds, the difference is treated as a gain or loss.

____9-35. If there are additional expenses incurred to dispose of the asset, these expenses are deducted from the proceeds in determining the gain or loss.

____9-36. When an asset is traded in to acquire a new asset of the same kind, the new asset may be recorded as the total of any cash paid plus the market value of the traded-in asset.

B. MULTIPLE CHOICE. Select the best response to each of the following, and mark the letter corresponding to your choice.

9-37. A company purchased machinery for $36,000. It was estimated to produce 16,000 units during its four-year life and to have a $4,000 salvage value. Using the sum-of-the-years'-digits method, what is depreciation expense in the first year?

    a. $14,400
    b. $10,800
    c. $12,800
    d. $ 9,600
    e. None of the above.

9-38.   A company purchased machinery for $36,000. It was estimated to produce 16,000 units during its four-year life and to have a $4,000 salvage value. Using the sum-of-the-years'-digits method, what is depreciation expense in the second year?

    a. $14,400
    b. $10,800
    c. $12,800
    d. $9,600
    e. None of the above.

9-39.   A company purchased machinery for $36,000. It was estimated to produce 16,000 units during its four-year life and to have a $4,000 salvage value. It produced 6,000 units during the first year. Using the units of production method, what is depreciation expense it the first year?

    a. $12,000
    b. $13,500
    c. $8,000
    d. $9,600
    e. None of the above.

9-40.   A company purchased machinery for $36,000. It was estimated to produce 16,000 units during its four-year life and to have a $4,000 salvage value. Using the double declining balance method, what is depreciation expense in the first year?

    a. $16,000
    b. $18,000
    c. $8,000
    d. $9,000
    e. None of the above.

9-41. A company purchased machinery for $36,000. It was estimated to produce 16,000 units during its four-year life and to have a $4,000 salvage value. Using the double declining balance method, what is depreciation expense in the second year?

    a. $16,000
    b. $18,000
    c. $8,000
    d. $9,000
    e. None of the above.

9-42. A company purchased machinery for $36,000. It was estimated to produce 16,000 units during its four-year life and to have a $4,000 salvage value. Using the double declining balance method, and assuming the machine was sold for $8,000 at the end of its second year, what was the gain (loss) on disposal?

    a.   ($2,000.)
    b. $2,000
    c. $1,000
    d.   ($1,000.)
    e. None of the above.

USE THIS INFORMATION FOR PROBLEMS 43- 48

A company had the following inventory purchases during the year:

Jan. 1	100 units @ $10	$1,000
Mar. 1	500 units @ $11	$5,500
Jun. 1	300 units @ $13	$3,900
Oct. 1	100 units @ $14	$1,400

9-43. If the ending inventory consists of 110 units, what is the cost of ending inventory assuming periodic LIFO?

    a. $1,530
    b. $1,540
    c. $1,110
    d. $1,400
    e. None of the above.

9-44. If the ending inventory consists of 110 units, what is the cost of goods sold assuming periodic LIFO?

    a. $10,270
    b. $10,260
    c. $10,690
    d. $10,400
    e. None of the above.

9-45. If the ending inventory consists of 110 units, what is the cost of ending inventory assuming average costing?

    a. $1,110
    b. $1,530
    c. $1,540
    d. $1,298
    e. None of the above.

9-46. If the ending inventory consists of 110 units, what is the cost of goods sold assuming average costing?

    a. $10,502
    b. $10,400
    c. $10,690
    d. $10,260
    e. None of the above.

9-47. If the ending inventory consists of 110 units, what is the cost of ending inventory assuming periodic FIFO?

    a. $1,530
    b. $1,540
    c. $1,110
    d. $1,400
    e. None of the above.

9-48. If the ending inventory consists of 110 units, what is the cost of goods sold assuming periodic FIFO?

    a. $10,270
    b. $10,260
    c. $10,690
    d. $10,400
    e. None of the above.

CHAPTER TEN

LIABILITY MEASUREMENT AND EXPENSE RECOGNITION

CHAPTER OUTLINE

LIABILITIES

1. Liabilities are obligations of the firm to external parties other than the owners.

2. There is usually a specified date by which the liability must be repaid.

3. Many liabilities require a future cash payment; some may be discharged by providing goods or services.

4. The value of a loan to the borrower is equal to the present value of the future payments to be made.

5. Unless there is an explicit charge for the use of the funds, the cost of funds may be ignored when the period of time between the acquisition of resources or money in a credit arrangement and its ultimate repayment is short.

6. There are two primary issues in accounting for liabilities.

   a. Allocating the cost of using the funds to the proper time periods over the life of the liability.

   b. Measuring the value of the liability to be disclosed on the balance sheet date.

7. In many cases the periodic cost of using borrowed funds is relatively straightforward and can be determined by multiplying the stated interest rate times the amount to be repaid.

8. However, transactions giving rise to the creation of a liability can involve more complex circumstances.

CORPORATE BONDS

1. Corporate bonds are typically issued at a premium or discount; that is, they are sold for more or less than face value.

2. The premium or discount occurs because there is a difference between the _interest rate on the bond contracts_ and the _market interest rate_ at the time of sale.

3. No matter what they actually pay for the bonds, buyers receive the periodic _cash payments_ stipulated by the _bond contract_ (that is, they receive the bond contract's _stated interest rate_ multiplied by the _face value_ of the bonds).

4. Buyers _adjust the price_ they are willing to pay for the bonds to assure themselves that they are receiving the _market rate_ on their investment. That is, they pay more or less than face value for the bonds, creating premiums or discounts.

5. Multiplying the bond contract rate by the face value on the bonds will tell you how much _cash_ the firm has to pay the bondholders each period, but it will NOT tell you _interest expense_ the firm is incurring because the calculation fails to take into account the premium or discount.

6. The effective interest rate method must be used to calculate interest expense.

The effective interest rate method.

1. The effective interest rate of a liability at the time it is issued is that interest rate at which the present value of the principal and interest payments to be made over the life of the liability exactly equals the proceeds to the borrower.

2. The effective interest rate is established by the market at the time the funds are borrowed and does NOT change, despite later changes in the market rate of interest.

3.   The effective interest rate can be determined by trial and error. (The process is described on page 245 in the text.)

4.   The effective interest rate is used to determine interest expense.

5.   To calculate interest expense multiply the present value of the liability at the beginning of the accounting period by the effective interest rate.

6.   If money is borrowed, the difference between what is borrowed (proceeds) and what is paid back is the interest.

7.   When the effective interest method is used, the total interest expense (recognized over the period of time the loan is being repaid) is equal to the difference between the proceeds and the amount repaid.

Carrying value of liability

1.   The liability is to be carried on the borrower's balance sheet at the present value of the remaining cash payments.

2.   Beginning balance of the liability
       + Interest expense
       - Cash payments
        Ending balance of the liability.

3.   If the market rate of interest remains at the original effective rate, the carrying value of the liability will equal the amount at which the bonds could be traded in the marketplace.

4.   If the market rate differs from the original effective rate, the market value of the bonds will not be the same as their carrying value.

5.   Many accountants prefer to use separate premium and discount accounts.   In such cases

   a. the cash account is debited for the amount received,
   b. the bonds payable account is credited for the face amount of the liability and
   c. a discount (premium) account is debited (credited) for the difference.

d. The carrying value of the bonds is simply:

$$\begin{array}{c}
\text{bonds payable} \\
\underline{-\text{ discount on bonds}} \\
\text{carrying value}
\end{array}
\quad \text{OR} \quad
\begin{array}{c}
\text{bonds payable} \\
\underline{+\text{premium on bonds}} \\
\text{carrying value}
\end{array}$$

6. If a separate discount or premium account is established,

   a. each time interest expense is recorded the balance in the discount or premium account is <u>reduced</u>;
   b. the amount in the bonds payable account is <u>not changed</u>.

7. At the maturity date of the bonds the balance in the discount or premium account is zero.

8. Thus, at maturity, the carrying value of the bonds equals the bond's principal amount (face value).

INSTALLMENT LIABILITIES

1. Note that the bond contracts discussed above require periodic cash payments representing interest; the principal amount is paid out all at once at maturity.

2. Generally, installment liabilities involve regular payments, each of which includes <u>both</u> interest and principal.

3. The principal repayment serves to reduce the carrying value of the liability.

RETIREMENT OF DEBT BEFORE MATURITY

1. At times prior to maturity the carrying value of a liability may differ from its current market value.

2. A firm may decide to retire the debt early.

3. If the debt is retired when there is a <u>difference</u> between its carrying value (on the books) and its market value (the amount at which it is actually retired), this difference is recognized as an <u>extraordinary gain or loss</u> in determining net income in the period in which the debt is retired.

DISCLOSURE OF LIABILITIES

1. For long-term liabilities it is useful to disclose the terms

(rates at which interest is paid on face amounts, dates that interest/principal payments are due, etc.)

2. This disclosure can be made on the face of the balance sheet if it is brief and uncomplicated; otherwise, a total can be shown on the face of the balance sheet, and the details can be disclosed in the footnotes.

CAPITALIZED LEASES

1. A popular way for firms to acquire resources is by long-term noncancelable leases.

2. A "lessor" owns the property being rented out; a "lessee" uses the rented property.

3. Certain long-term noncancelable leases are in substance the purchase of an asset by the lessee (buyer), in which the lessor (seller) extends credit to the buyer.

4. The accounting treatment of a lease must reflect the economic substance (rather than the legal form) of the transaction.

Lessee

1. If the lessee judges a lease to be in substance a purchase, the following must be recognized at the date of the transaction:

   a. The credit arrangement results in a liability which is recorded at the present value of the future lease payments;

   b. The lessee also gains control over an asset; this asset is also recorded at the present value of the lease payments.

2. As a result of the lease arrangement the lessee incurs two on-going expenses.

   a. The expense of USING the leased asset is recognized as depreciation of the initial asset value over the period the asset is used.

   b. The expense of FINANCING the asset is recognized as interest expense each period; the expense is calculated by multiplying the interest rate by the present value of the liability (remaining lease payments).

Lessor

1. If the lessor judges a lease to be in substance a <u>sale</u>, the following must be recorded at the <u>date of the transaction</u>:

    a. The <u>revenue</u> (at the present value of the future lease payments to be received);

    b. The lease payments receivable <u>asset</u> (equal to the present value of the future lease payments);

    c. The cost of goods sold <u>expense</u> (equal to the unexpired cost of the asset to the lessor);

    d. The <u>disposal</u> of the asset.

2. During the term of the lease:

    a. Interest earned is recognized as <u>financing revenue</u> in each period;

    b. The "lease payments receivable" account:

        i.   is increased by the interest earned on the present value of the remaining payments to be received;

        ii. is decreased by payments received from the lessee.

OPERATING LEASES

1. These are short-term rentals of assets.

2. The lessee records rental expense.

3. The lessor keeps the leased assets on its books and records:

    a. Rental revenue and

    b. Depreciation expense.

Distinguishing capital and operating leases

1. Determining whether a lease is an operating lease or requires capitalization is often difficult.

2. The FASB had indicated that the presence of ANY ONE of the following criteria would require the capitalization method.

    a. Title passes to the lessee;

    b. The lessee can purchase the leased asset at the end of the lease term for substantially less than its fair market value (a bargain purchase option);

    c. The lease term is at least 75 percent of the economic life of the leased asset;

    d. The present value of the lease payments is at least 90 percent of the fair market value of the leased asset.

INCOME TAXES

Financial accounting income versus tax accounting income

1. A firm's tax <u>liability</u> is based on the Internal Revenue Code.

2. Certain kinds of revenue and expenses, although included in <u>accounting income</u>, are NOT included in <u>taxable income</u>.

3. These items are a matter of national tax policy and create <u>permanent</u> differences because they will never become a part of taxable income.

4. In addition, <u>taxable income</u> may differ from <u>accounting income</u> due to permitted (legally and morally accepted) <u>timing</u> differences.

5. Timing differences arise if management chooses to use different measurement rules for tax and financial accounting purposes. (For example, management may choose to use different depreciation methods for financial accounting and tax accounting.)

6. Timing differences eventually reverse and cancel each other.

7. Thus, in the <u>absence of permanent differences between accounting income and tax income, over the life of the entity the sum of taxable income will equal the sum of accounting income.</u>

Income tax expense

1. If <u>financial accounting</u> income and <u>taxable</u> income differ in a given period, an issue arises about how to measure income tax expense. Should the expense be based on the financial accounting income or the taxable income?

2. Note that there is no choice as to the <u>liability</u>; it must be based on <u>taxable income</u>.

3. Those who support basing the <u>tax expense</u> on <u>taxable income</u> take a period-cost view of the issue.

4. Those who support basing the <u>tax expense</u> on <u>financial accounting income</u> argue for interperiod tax allocation.

The period-cost interpretation.

1. Those who support this view contend that the income tax <u>expense</u> recognized in a period should be <u>equal</u> to the amount of tax <u>liability</u> calculated based on taxable income of the period .

2. Advocates of this position argue that the income taxes paid (or payable) represent expenses of the period because they are assessed according to the taxable income of a given period.

3. Using this approach both the liability and the expense are calculated using the same measurement rules; consequently, the amounts for each item are the same.

4. The journal entry is simply:

        Income tax expense
            Income taxes payable

Interperiod tax allocation.

1. Those who support interperiod tax allocation contend that income tax expense should be based on <u>financial accounting income.</u>

2. If the <u>tax liability</u> is based on <u>taxable income</u> but the <u>tax expense</u> is based on <u>financial accounting income</u>, there will be a discrepancy between the two items (assuming the presence of timing differences).

3. The account created to handle this discrepancy is "deferred income taxes".

4. If the income tax expense is greater than the income tax liability, "deferred income taxes" is credited.

5. If the income tax liability is greater than the income tax expense, "deferred income taxes" is debited.

Income Tax Accounting Controversies

1. In addition to the argument described above (whether to base the income tax expense on financial accounting income or taxable income), there are additional areas of controversy.

2. Some advocates of interperiod allocation contend that income taxes should be allocated to future periods only when they are expected to reverse. This is difficult to predict with certainty as it depends on such events as the rate at which the business purchases new assets.

3. Another controvery involves the appropriate tax rate to use in establishing the deferred taxes.

   a. Some argue that the current tax rate should be used, even though the deferral will not reverse until some point in the future because future tax rates are not certain.

   b. Others argue that if future tax rates are available, they should be used.

4. **Current accounting policy** requires

   a. That interperiod tax allocation be used.

   b. That the tax rate of the period when the timing difference originates be used.

5. A recent accounting standard

   a. Requires that deferred income taxes be determined using enacted tax rates applicable to future years;

   b. Has been postponed to fiscal years beginning after December 15, 1990, due to complexities in applying the procedures.

PENSIONS

1. Benefits of pension plans depend on a number of factors: employee's age, compensation, length of employment, amount of contributions to the plan, and so forth.

2. Pension plans have recently become a major component of employee compensation and represent significant expenditures and obligations for firms.

Pension Assets and Liabilities

1. Companies typically deposit cash annually with an independent pension trustee.

2. The pension trustee is responsible for investing the cash and paying retirees their benefits.

3.   Cash contributions made by the firm (and possibly by employees)
   + the earnings from investing the cash
   - <u>the benefits paid to retirees</u>
       balance in the pension plan asset (held by the trustee)

4. The pension plan asset <u>also</u> has a fair market value which equals the market value of the securities the trustee has purchased with the cash not needed to pay benefits currently.

5. A company also has a pension <u>liability</u> to pay the benefits promised.

   a. Theoretically, the pension obligation is the present value of all the future payments to be made under the pension plan.

   b. However, to calculate the liability a number of assumptions must be made (number of years of employee service, longevity, salaries at retirement, an approriate interest rate, and so forth).

6. The FASB requires measurement of

   a. The **accumulated** benefit obligation based on current and past compensation levels

   b. The **projected** benefit obligation based on future compensation levels.

Pension cost

1. The intent is to measure pension cost over the time period in which the employee is in <u>active service</u> to the company.

2. The FASB has identified six components to be evaluated in calculation of the pension cost to be recognized in a period.

    a. <u>Service cost</u>: the benefits attributed by the pension plan to employee service during the period.
    b. <u>Interest cost</u>: the increase in the present value of the pension liability (measured as the PROJECTED benefit obligation) due to the passage of time.
    c. <u>Actual return on plan assets</u>: the change in the fair market value of the plan assets during the period.
    d. <u>Prior service cost</u>: a portion of the cost of retroactive benefits given in plan amendments to current and former employees for increased benefits based on services rendered in prior periods.
    e. <u>Gains or losses</u>: due to changes in the assumptions underlying the valuation of the plan asset or pension liability.
    f. A portion of the <u>transition amount</u> that was calculated when SFAS No. 87 was adopted.

3. The six components determine the amount <u>debited</u> by the employer to <u>pension expense</u>.

Balance sheet recognition

1. The employer's <u>cash contributions</u> to the pension fund do NOT necessarily equal the amount calculated as <u>pension expense</u>.

2. The <u>contributions</u> to the pension fund determine the amount <u>credited</u> to the <u>cash</u> account.

3. If the company contributes more cash to the fund than the amount calculated as pension expense, the difference is debited to an asset account "<u>prepaid pension cost</u>".

4. If the company contributes less cash to the fund than the amount calculated as pension expense, the difference is credited to a liability account "<u>unfunded accrued pension cost</u>".

5. In addition, at the end of the period the company must compare the amount of the accumulated benefit obligation and the fair

market value of the pension plan assets (which are held by the trustee).

a. If the fair market value of the plan assets is less than the accumulated benefit obligation, the company must recognize a <u>liability for the difference.</u>

b. If the fair market value of the plan assets is more than the accumulated benefit obligation, the company <u>may NOT recognize an asset for the difference</u>.

QUESTIONS AND EXERCISES

A. TRUE-FALSE. Indicate whether each of the following statements is true or false.

_____10-1. Liabilities are obligations of the firm to external parties and the owners.

_____10-2. There is usually (but not always) a specified date by which the liability must be repaid.

_____10-3. Many (not all) liabilities require a future cash payment; some may be discharged by providing goods or services.

_____10-4. Unless there is an explicit charge for the use of the funds, the cost of funds may be ignored when the period of time between the acquisition of resources or money in a credit arrangement and its ultimate repayment is short.

_____10-5. Allocating the cost of using the funds to the proper time periods over the life of the liability is an accounting issue but measuring the value of the liability to be disclosed on the balance sheet date is not.

_____10-6. Corporate bonds are always issued at face value initially.

_____10-7. The cash payments received by bond buyers depend on the amount actually paid for the bonds.

____10-8. No matter what they pay for the bonds, buyers receive periodic cash payments based on the market interest rate multiplied by the face value of the bonds.

____10-9. No matter what they pay for the bonds, buyers receive periodic cash payments based on the stated interest rate multiplied by the market value of the bonds.

____10-10. Buyers adjust the price they are willing to pay for the bonds to assure themselves that they are receiving the market rate on their investment.

____10-11. Multiplying the bond contract rate by the face value on the bonds will tell you how much cash the firm has to pay the bondholders each period.

____10-12. Multiplying the bond contract rate by the face value on the bonds will NOT tell you the interest expense the firm is incurring.

____10-13. The effective interest rate of a liability at the time it is issued is that interest rate at which the present value of the principal payments to be made over the life of the liability exactly equals the proceeds to the borrower.

____10-14. The effective interest rate is established by the market at the time the funds are borrowed, but it changes along with future changes in the market rate of interest.

____10-15. The coupon interest rate is used to determine interest expense.

____10-16. To calculate interest expense multiply the present value of the liability as of the beginning of the accounting period by the effective interest rate.

____10-17. To calculate interest expense multiply the present value of the liability as of the beginning of the accounting period by the bond contract interest rate.

____10-18. Even if, in the years following the issuance of bonds, the market rate of interest differs from the rate that was in effect when the bonds were issued, the carrying value of the liability on the balance sheet will still equal the amount at which the bonds could be traded in the marketplace.

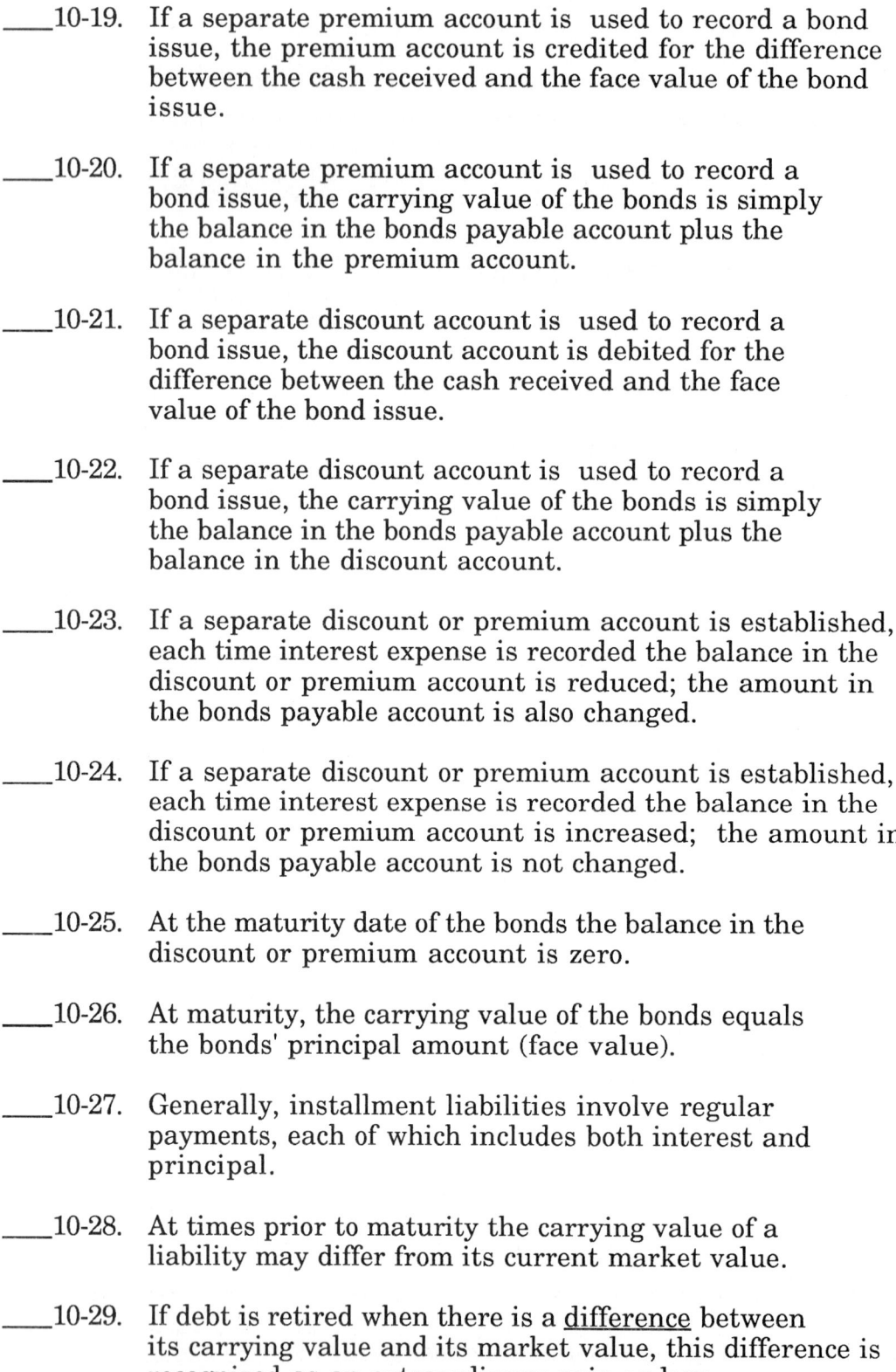

_____10-19. If a separate premium account is used to record a bond issue, the premium account is credited for the difference between the cash received and the face value of the bond issue.

_____10-20. If a separate premium account is used to record a bond issue, the carrying value of the bonds is simply the balance in the bonds payable account plus the balance in the premium account.

_____10-21. If a separate discount account is used to record a bond issue, the discount account is debited for the difference between the cash received and the face value of the bond issue.

_____10-22. If a separate discount account is used to record a bond issue, the carrying value of the bonds is simply the balance in the bonds payable account plus the balance in the discount account.

_____10-23. If a separate discount or premium account is established, each time interest expense is recorded the balance in the discount or premium account is reduced; the amount in the bonds payable account is also changed.

_____10-24. If a separate discount or premium account is established, each time interest expense is recorded the balance in the discount or premium account is increased; the amount in the bonds payable account is not changed.

_____10-25. At the maturity date of the bonds the balance in the discount or premium account is zero.

_____10-26. At maturity, the carrying value of the bonds equals the bonds' principal amount (face value).

_____10-27. Generally, installment liabilities involve regular payments, each of which includes both interest and principal.

_____10-28. At times prior to maturity the carrying value of a liability may differ from its current market value.

_____10-29. If debt is retired when there is a <u>difference</u> between its carrying value and its market value, this difference is recognized as an extraordinary gain or loss.

____10-30. A lessee never records leased property as an asset because the property is not owned by the lessee.

____10-31. Operating leases are short-term rentals of assets.

____10-32. If a lease contract contains a bargain purchase option, it is an operating lease.

____10-33. If a lease contract indicates that the lease term is at least 75 percent of the economic life of the leased asset, it is an operating lease.

____10-34. Certain kinds of revenue and expenses, although included in accounting income, are not included in taxable income.

____10-35. Although tax timing differences are technically legal, they are not considered to be very ethical by the accounting profession.

____10-36. Timing differences arise if management chooses to use different measurement rules for tax and financial accounting purposes.

____10-37. Permanent differences arise if management chooses to use different measurement rules for tax and financial accounting purposes.

____10-38. If financial accounting income and taxable income differ in a given period, an issue arises about how to measure income tax expense.

____10-39. Those who support interperiod tax allocation contend that income tax expense should be based on taxable accounting income.

____10-40. If the income tax expense is greater than the income tax liability, "deferred income taxes" is credited.

____10-41. If the income tax liability is greater than the income tax expense, "deferred income taxes" is debited.

____10-42. Some argue that the current tax rate should be used to allocate income taxes (even though the deferral will not reverse until some point in the future) because future tax rates are not certain.

____10-43. A recent accounting standard, the application of which has been postponed, requires that deferred income taxes be determined using current tax rates.

____10-44. The balance in the pension plan asset (held by the trustee) is equal to the cash contributions made by the firm (and possibly by employees) plus the earnings from investing the cash minus the benefits paid to retirees.

____10-45. As defined by the FASB the accumulated benefit obligation is based on future compensation levels

____10-46. As defined by the FASB the projected benefit obligation is based on future compensation levels.

____10-47. The intent of pension accounting is to measure pension cost over the time period in which the employee is in active service to the company (rather than the time period in which she collects benefits).

____10-48. The six components of pension cost determine the amount debited by the employer to pension expense.

____10-49. "Service cost" equals the benefits attributed by the pension plan to employee service for the period.

____10-50. The "actual return on plan assets" is the change in the fair market value of the plan assets during the period.

____10-51. Changes in the assumptions underlying the valuation of the plan assets or pension liability may produce gains and/or losses.

____10-52. If the company contributes more cash to the fund than the amount calculated as pension expense, the difference is debited to an asset account "prepaid pension cost".

____10-53. If, at the end of the period, the fair market value of the pension plan assets (which are held by the trustee), exceeds the amount of the accumulated benefit obligation the company is permitted to recognize an asset for the difference.

B. MULTIPLE CHOICE - Select the best response to each of the following, and mark the letter corresponding to your choice.

10-54. Which of the following statements is FALSE?

   a. No matter what they pay for the bonds, buyers receive periodic cash payments based on the stated interest rate multiplied by the market value of the bonds.

   b. Buyers adjust the price they are willing to pay for the bonds to assure themselves that they are receiving the market rate on their investment.

   c. Multiplying the bond contract rate by the face value on the bonds will tell you how much cash the firm has to pay the bondholders each period.

   d. Multiplying the bond contract rate by the face value on the bonds will NOT tell you the interest expense the firm is incurring.

   e. The effective interest rate of a liability at the time it is issued is that interest rate at which the present value of the principal and interest payments to be made over the life of the liability exactly equals the proceeds to the borrower.

10-55. Which of the following statements is FALSE?

   a. A recent accounting standard, the application of which has been postponed, requires that deferred income taxes be determined using current tax rates.

   b. The balance in the pension plan asset (held by the trustee) is equal to the cash contributions made by the firm (and possibly by employees) plus the earnings from investing the cash minus the benefits paid to retirees.

   c. As defined by the FASB the accumulated benefit obligation is based on current and compensation levels

   d. As defined by the FASB the projected benefit obligation is based on future compensation levels.

   e. The intent of pension accounting is to measure pension cost over the time period in which the employee is in active service to the company (rather than the time period in which she collects benefits).

10-56. A company issued five-year bonds with a total face value of $50,000 and a stated interest rate of 8 percent. As the market rate of interest was 10 percent, the bonds sold at a discount of $3,790. What was the carrying value of the bonds at date of issue?

    a. $50,000
    b. $53,790
    c. $46,210
    d. None of the above.

10-57. A company issued five-year bonds with a total face value of $50,000 and a stated interest rate of 8 percent. As the market rate of interest was 10 percent, the bonds sold at a discount of $3,790. At the first payment date, the company must pay the bondholders cash of:

    a. $4,000
    b. $5,000
    c. $4,621
    d. $3,697
    e. None of the above.

10-58. A company issued five-year bonds with a total face value of $50,000 and a stated interest rate of 8 percent. As the market rate of interest was 10 percent, the bonds sold at a discount of $3,790. At the end of the first accounting period, the company must record interest expense of:

    a. $4,000
    b. $5,000
    c. $4,621
    d. $3,697
    e. None of the above

10-59. A company issued five-year bonds with a total face value of $50,000 and a stated interest rate of 8 percent. As the market rate of interest was 10 percent, the bonds sold at a discount of $3,790. At the end of the first accounting period, the carrying value of the bonds is:

    a. $50,000
    b. $46,210
    c. $46,831
    d. $46,000
    e. None of the above.

10-60. A company issued five-year bonds with a total face value of $50,000 and a stated interest rate of 8 percent. As the market rate of interest was 10 percent, the bonds sold at a discount of $3,790. At the end of the SECOND accounting period, the company must record interest expense of:

    a. $4,000
    b. $4,621
    c. $5,000
    d. $4,683
    e. None of the above.

CHAPTER ELEVEN

RECOGNITION OF OWNERSHIP INTERESTS

CHAPTER OUTLINE

OWNERS' EQUITY

1. Paid-in capital is that portion of owners' equity representing the assets contributed by the owners for their ownership interests.

2. Retained earnings is that portion of owners' equity representing the cumulative excess of net income over dividend distribution or withdrawals.

3. The claims of creditors are legally protected by restricting the dividends paid to owners to the balance in retained earnings.

Classifications of Paid-in Capital

1. A company may issue various classes of stock.

   a. Owners of common stock generally have the right to

      i. Vote for members of the board of directors and (in some states) vote on certain types of major corporate decisions;

      ii. Share proportionally in dividends declared;

      iii. Share proportionally in the net assets of the firm if the corporation is liquidated.

   b. Other classes of stock may

      i. be given preference over common stock on certain rights; and/or

ii. forfeit one or more of the other rights

c. Typically, owners of preferred stock

   i. have preference over common shareholders as to dividend or liquidation distribution;

   ii. but forfeit voting rights;

d. Often the dividend preference for preferred stock owners is cumulative.

e. Preferred stock may also be participating (share with common shareholders any dividend distributions exceeding the preferred shareholders stipulated dividend rate).

f. Some preferred stock also has a conversion right which entitles the shareholder to convert the preferred stock into a specified number of shares of common stock.

2. Many states require corporations to specify a value for each share of stock, referred to as the <u>par value</u> or <u>stated value</u> of the stock.

a. Corporations cannot sell their stock for less than par value or stated value.

b. The par value or stated value was intended to provide a buffer to protect the claims of nonowners against the corporation.

c. However, par or stated value can be very low and, in some states no-par stock may be issued.

d. The real security for the creditors is provided by the actual asset values and related earning power of the corporation.

e. If the company's stock has a par or stated value, paid-in capital is divided into two categories.

   i. Common stock, par value
   ii. Paid-in capital in excess of par value

Dividends

1. Cash dividends

   a. Dividends must be formally authorized by the board of directors of a corporation.

   b. On the <u>declaration date</u> the total dividend to be paid becomes a binding liability. This is generally recorded by a debit to retained earnings and a credit to dividends payable.

   c. At the <u>date of record</u> owners holding the stock establish their right to receive dividends.

   d. On the <u>payment date</u> the dividends payable account is debited and the cash account is credited.

2. Stock dividends

   a. Sometimes a firm declares dividends payable in shares of stock; this is called a stock dividend.

   b. Although each shareholder has more shares of stock in the corporation after the stock dividend, each individual's proportionate share of ownership is unchanged.

   c. If the stock dividend is small (less than 25% of the outstanding shares),

      i. the market price of each share of stock seldom adjusts downward sufficiently to offset the increase in the number of shares outstanding;

      ii. thus, the shareholders receive income equal to the market value of the stock received in the dividend;

      iii. therefore, the company records the stock dividend using the <u>fair market value</u> of the stock.

          Retained earnings
              Common stock, par value
              Paid-in capital in excess of par

144

d. If the stock dividend is more than 25% of the outstanding shares,

   i. it is likely that the market price of all the shares will adjust downward to reflect the greater supply of stock;

   ii. the stock dividend is recorded at the par or stated value of the stock.

   Retained earnings
       Common stock-par value

Stock splits

1. These are sometimes used as a means of increasing the number of shares outstanding in order to reduce the market price per share, presumably making the company's stock more easily purchased.

2. The old shares of stock are called in by the corporation.

3. New shares are issued with a different (usually lower) par value.

4. The total amount of legal capital is unchanged.

5. No journal entries are required for a stock split.

Treasury stock

1. Firms sometimes repurchase some of their stock in the open market or directly from shareholders; if stock is not cancelled but held for reissue, it is called treasury stock.

2. Stocks repurchased and held for resale are not considered assets.

3. The firm receives no dividends and records no dividend revenue on its treasury stock.

4. The total cost of the treasury stock is treated as a reduction of owners' equity.

5. If the treasury stock is subsequently sold, the corporation does not record a gain or loss; any difference between the cost of the treasury stock and the proceeds from the sale is recorded in paid-in capital in excess of par.

Stock options

1. A stock option is a legal instrument permitting the holder to acquire a specified number of shares of stock at a specified price.

2. Typically, options are valid for a limited period of time and are not transferable.

3. If a firm has issued stock options, it must disclose the potential number of new shares that may be issued.

4. Options are often issued as a form of executive compensation.

5. The amount of compensation expense that should be recognized is the difference between the price that must be paid for the stock if the options are exercised and the fair market value of the stock <u>on the date the options are granted</u>.

6. The compensation expense should be recognized as an expense in future period(s).

INTERCORPORATE INVESTMENTS

1. Corporations may own stock in other companies.

2. Accounting for stock ownership of other firms depends on the degree of ownership.

Lower-of-cost-or-market method - (0-20% ownership)

1. Minimal ownership indicates that the investment represents a temporary use of excess cash.

2. This is initally recorded as an investment in marketable securities at cost.

3. Since there is no guarantee of the amount that would be received were the stocks sold, the portfolio of marketable equity securities is accounted for using the lower-of-cost-or-market method.

   a. If the market value of the portfolio is less than its cost, the portfolio is shown at market and a loss is recorded;

   b. If the portfolio is a current asset, such a loss is recognized

146

in the current period's income statement;

c. If the portfolio is a noncurrent asset, such a loss is recorded as a debit to an owners' equity account "unrealized loss on noncurrent marketable securities".

d. In either case, an allowance account (contra asset) is used to reduce the balance in the intercorporate investment account.

e. Dividends are recognized as income at the time they are declared by the investee.

f. When the shares are sold, the difference between the carrying value and the proceeds is recognized as a gain or loss.

Equity method - (20-50% ownership)

1. Investment at this level indicates that the investor firm has a more permanent investment intent.

2. The investment is initially recorded at cost.

3. A comparison is made between the amount paid for the stock and the investor's percentage ownership of the investee's net assets (at book value); any difference between the two amounts will be amortized in future periods.

4. Each period the investor company recognizes its percentage share of the investee's net income.

   a. The asset account (Investment in Investee Company) is increased (debited) by the appropriate amount.

   b. The amount is also recognized by the investor as income for the period.

5. Each period any necessary amortization (see item 3)

   a. reduces the investment account and

   b. appears on the income statement

6. As dividends are declared by the investee

   a. The dividends receivable (or cash) account is increased (debited);

b. The investment account is reduced (credited);

c. Note that dividends REDUCE the asset account and do NOT appear on the income statement; the investor's share of the investee's earnings are recognized by the investor as the investee generates income; dividends are treated as a return of the investment in the form of cash.

Consolidation (50% or greater ownership)

1. Once an investor has acquired 50% or more of an investee, consolidated financial statements must be prepared for the combined firms.

2. The investor is now called the "parent" and the investee is referred to as the "subsidiary".

3. Each company continues to maintain its own set of books.

4. The process of consolidation is done only for the financial statements; the two sets of books remain.

5. To consolidate the two firms' statements one essentially adds together all the like accounts (e.g., parent's cash + subsidiary's cash = consolidated firm's cash; parent's revenues + subsidiary's revenues = consolidated revenues, etc.).

6. However, certain steps must be taken

a. to avoid double counting;

b. to account for minority interest (the portion of the subsidiary NOT owned by the parent); and

c. to achieve appropriate classification on the consolidated statements.

7. To consolidate **balance sheets** the following procedures are necessary

a. Array all balance sheet accounts of the parent and subsidiary side-by-side (see Exhibit 11-7 in the text on page 292).

b. Since a single entity (the consolidated firm) cannot own itself, the parent's "Investment in Investee" account must be eliminated;

c. A portion of the total balance in the "Investment in Investee" account may NOT be a claim by the parent against the net assets of the subsidiary IF the parent paid more than book value for the stock. If this has occurred, the amount paid in excess of book value must be set up in a separate asset account on the consolidated statements as "Excess of investment cost over equity acquired in net assets of Subsidiary (this amount will be amortized in future periods);

d. The subsidiary's paid-in capital and retained earnings must be eliminated;

e. If the parent does not own 100% of the subsidiary, a "minority interest" account must be created for the portion not owned.

f. After all eliminations and reclassifications are accomplished, the accounts are then combined for the consolidated balance sheet.

7. Parent and subsidiary **income statements** are NOT combined at date of acquisition because the companies have not operated for a period as related companies.

8. To combine **income statements** subsequent to acquisition

a. Array the income statements of the parent and subsidiary side-by-side (see Exhibit 11-9 on page 294 in the text).

b. Since all of subsidiary's revenue and expenses are brought into the consolidation through its own statement, the "Equity in Subsidiary Earnings" on the parent's own statement is redundant; to avoid double counting it is eliminated;

c. The minority interest in the subsidiary's net income must be eliminated from the combined accounts;

d. The parent's "amortization of the excess of cost of investment over interest in net assets of subsidiary" must be reclassified so that in the combined statements it appears with the depreciation and amortization of other assets of the combined companies;

e. After all eliminations and reclassifications are accomplished, the accounts are then combined for the consolidated income statement.

9. Note that the **consolidated net income** figure **equals** the **parent company's separate net income** figure.

   a. Under the equity method (parent only statements) the income of the parent includes its percentage share of subsidiary net earnings as a single figure added to income.

   b. In consolidated statements, rather than adding a single total figure (the percentage share of subsidiary net earnings) to the rest of the parent's income, each of the individual revenue and expense accounts of the combined companies are added together (after appropriate eliminations, reclassifications, and accounting for minority interests); either process should produce the same final amount of net income.

10. When a parent company purchases stock in subsidiaries by issuing parent company stock in the exchange (rather than using cash or other consideration), a controversy arises because of the alternative ways in which the transaction can be interpreted.

   a. One view is that the exchange is a purchase, in that the parent could have sold their stock for cash and then used the cash to invest in the subsidiary.

      1. Under this interpretation, the accounting is as described above.

      2. The investment in the subsidiary is recorded at the market value of the parent stock issued in exchange for it.

   b. Alternatively, the exchange can be viewed as a **pooling** of the interests of the shareholders of the parent and those of the subsidiary.

      1. In this case the accounting used is the pooling-of-interest method.

      2. The investment is recorded at an amount equal to the equity acquired by the parent in the subsidiary's net assets.

      3. The subsidiary's assets continue to be carried at their book value.

4.   Even when the acquisition price exceeds the book value of the acquired entity, no additional amortization expense is offset against the postacquisition combined income of the parent and subsidiary.

5.   Thus, the combined income will be higher subsequent to acquisition under pooling of interests than under the purchase method of accounting. This has led to widespread abuses.

QUESTIONS AND EXERCISES

A. TRUE-FALSE. Indicate whether each of the following statements is true or false.

_____11-1.   Owners of common stock generally have the right to vote for members of the board of directors and (in some states) to vote on certain types of major corporate decisions.

_____11-2.   Owners of common stock generally have the right to share proportionally in dividends declared.

_____11-3.   Owners of common stock generally have the right to share proportionally in the net assets of the firm if the corporation is liquidated.

_____11-4.   Typically, owners of preferred stock have preference over common shareholders as to liquidation distribution.

_____11-5.   Often the dividend preference for preferred stock owners is cumulative.

_____11-6.   Preferred stock is never participating (never shares with common shareholders any dividend distributions exceeding the preferred shareholders stipulated dividend rate).

_____11-7. Preferred stock can also have a conversion right which entitles the shareholder to convert the preferred stock into a specified number of shares of common stock.

_____11-8. Many states require corporations to specify a value for each share of stock, referred to as the par value or stated value of the stock.

_____11-9. The par value or stated value provides real security to protect the claims of nonowners against the corporation.

_____11-10. Par value is a guarantee to stockholders that the value of their stock will never fall below the specified par.

_____11-11. Par or stated value can be very low and, in some states no-par stock may be issued.

_____11-12. The actual asset values and related earning power of the corporation provide more real security for the creditors than par values do.

_____11-13. Although each shareholder has more shares of stock in the corporation after a stock dividend, each individual's proportionate share of ownership is unchanged.

_____11-14. If the stock dividend is more than 25% of the outstanding shares, it is likely that the market price of all the shares will adjust downward to reflect the greater supply of stock.

_____11-15. If the stock dividend is more than 25% of the outstanding shares, the stock dividend is recorded at the par or stated value of the stock.

_____11-16. Treasury stocks are not considered assets.

_____11-17. The firm receives no dividends and records no dividend revenue on its treasury stock.

_____11-18. The total cost of treasury stock is treated as a reduction of owners' equity.

_____11-19. If treasury stock is subsequently sold, the corporation records a gain or loss as the difference between the cost of the treasury stock and the proceeds from the sale.

____11-20. When a firm issues stock options as a form of executive compensation, the amount of compensation expense that should be recognized is the difference between the price that must be paid for the stock if the options are exercised and the fair market value of the stock on the date the options are granted.

____11-21. When a firm issues stock options as a form of executive compensation, the compensation expense should be recognized as an expense in the period in which the options are issued.

____11-22. Corporations may not own stock in other companies.

____11-23. Accounting for stock ownership of other firms depends on the degree of ownership.

____11-24. When a firm accounts for an investment in stock using the lower-of-cost-or-market method, dividends are recognized as income at the time they are declared by the investee.

____11-25. Assuming that a firm accounts for an investment in stock using the lower-of-cost-or-market method, when the shares are sold, the difference between the carrying value and the proceeds is recognized as a gain or loss.

____11-26. Typically, the equity method of accounting is used when a firm owns 20-50% of the common stock of another company.

____11-27. Under the equity method of accounting for investments in the stock of other corporations, as dividends are declared by the investee, the dividends receivable (or cash) account is increased (debited) and the investment account is reduced (credited).

____11-28. When the equity method of accounting for investments in the common stock of other firms is used, the payment of dividends by the investee reduces the asset (investment account).

____11-29. When the equity method of accounting for investments in the common stock of other firms is used, the payment of dividends by the investee has no effect on the income statement.

____11-30. When the equity method of accounting for investments in the common stock of other firms is used, the investor's share of the investee's earnings is recognized by the investor as the investee generates income.

____11-31. When the equity method of accounting for investments in the common stock of other firms is used, the receipt of dividends is treated as a return of the investment in the form of cash.

____11-32. Once an investor has acquired 50% or more of an investee, consolidated financial statements may be prepared for the combined firms, but consolidation is not required.

____11-33. Once a "parent" has purchased enough stock in another firm to turn it into a "subsidiary", the subsidiary closes its accounting records and all subsequent transactions and events are recorded only on the parent's books.

____11-34. If a parent firm has purchased 70% of the stock of a subsidiary firm, the two income statements must be consolidated at date of acquisition.

____11-35. In consolidating income statements subsequent to acquistion, the "Equity in Subsidiary Earnings" account on the parent's statement is eliminated from the combined accounts.

____11-36. In consolidating income statements subsequent to acquisition, the minority interest in the subsidiary's net income must be eliminated from the combined accounts.

____11-37. In consolidating income statements subsequent to acquisition, the parent's "amortization of the excess of cost of investment over interest in net assets of subsidiary" must be reclassified so that in the combined statements it appears with the depreciation and amortization of other assets of the combined companies.

154

____11-38. The consolidated net income figure equals the parent company's separate net income figure.

____11-39. Under the equity method (parent only statements) the income of the parent includes its percentage share of subsidiary net earnings as a single figure added to income.

____11-40. In consolidated statements, rather than adding a single total figure (the percentage share of subsidiary net earnings) to the rest of the parent's income, each of the individual revenue and expense accounts of the combined companies are added together (after appropriate eliminations, reclassifications, and accounting for minority interests).

____11-41. When a parent company purchases stock in a subsidiary by issuing parent company stock in the exchange, if the transaction is viewed as a purchase, the investment in the subsidiary is recorded at the book value of the parent stock issued in exchange for it.

____11-42. When a parent company purchases stock in a subsidiary by issuing parent company stock in the exchange, if the transaction is viewed as a pooling of the interests of the shareholders of the parent and those of the subsidiary, the investment is recorded at an amount equal to the book value of the equity acquired by the parent in the subsidiary's net assets.

____11-43. In a parent-subsidiary combination accounted for as a pooling, the subsidiary's assets continue to be carried at their book value.

____11-44. In a parent-subsidiary combination accounted for as a pooling, even when the acquisition price exceeds the book value of the acquired entity, no additional amortization expense is offset against the postacquisition combined income of the parent and subsidiary.

____11-45. In a parent-subsidiary combination, the combined income subsequent to acquisition will be higher under pooling of interests accounting than under the purchase method of accounting.

155

11-46. Which of the following statements is TRUE?

    a. Retained earnings is that portion of owners' equity representing the assets contributed by the owners for their ownership interests.

    b. Paid-in capital is that portion of owners' equity representing the cumulative excess of net income over dividend distribution or withdrawals.

    c. The claims of creditors are legally protected by restricting the dividends paid to owners to the balance in retained earnings.

    d. All of the above are true.

    e. None of the above is true.

11-47. Typically, owners of preferred stock

    a. have preference over common shareholders as to dividend distribution;

    b. do not have preference over common shareholders as to liquidation distribution;

    c. have full voting rights;

    d. none of the above.

11-48. Which of the following is true with respect to cash dividends

    a. Dividends may be formally authorized by the managers of a corporation.

    b. On the declaration date the total dividend to be paid becomes a binding liability. This is recorded by a debit to retained earnings and a credit to dividends payable.

    c. At the payment date owners holding the stock establish their right to receive dividends.

    d. On the date of record the dividends payable account is debited and the cash account is credited.

11-49. If a stock dividend is small (less than 25% of the outstanding shares),

    a. The market price of each share of stock seldom adjusts downward sufficiently to offset the increase in the number of shares outstanding.
    b. The shareholders receive income equal to the market value of the stock received in the dividend.
    c. The company records the stock dividend using the fair market value of the stock.
    d. All of the above are true.

11-50. Which of the following statements is FALSE with respect to stock splits?

    a. These are sometimes used as a means of increasing the number of shares outstanding in order to reduce the market price per share, presumably making the company's stock more easily purchased.
    b. The old shares of stock are called in by the corporation.
    c. New shares are issued with a different (usually lower) par value.
    d. The total amount of legal capital is changed.
    e. No journal entries are required for a stock split.

11-51. Which of the following is FALSE with respect to stock options?

    a. A stock option is a legal instrument permitting the holder to acquire a specified number of shares of stock at a specified price.
    b. Typically, options are valid for an unlimited period of time and are not transferable.
    c. If a firm has issued stock options, it must disclose the potential number of new shares that may be issued.
    d. Options are often issued as a form of executive compensation.

11-52. Assume a firm purchases 4% of the common stock of another company and records the purchase as an investment in marketable securities at cost. Which statement is TRUE with respect to accounting for that purchase?

    a. If, at the balance sheet date, the market value of the investment portfolio is less than its cost, the portfolio is shown at market and a loss is recorded.

    b. If the portfolio is a current asset, such a loss is recognized in the current period's income statement;

    c. If the portfolio is a noncurrent asset, such a loss is recorded as a debit to an owners' equity account "unrealized loss on noncurrent marketable securities".

    d. In either case, an allowance account (contra asset) is used to reduce the balance in the intercorporate investment account.

    e. All of the above statements are true.

11-53. Assume a firm purchases 45% of the common stock of another company. Which statement is FALSE with respect to accounting for that purchase?

    a. The investment is initially recorded at cost.

    b. A comparison is made between the amount paid for the stock and the investor's percentage ownership of the investee's net assets (at book value); any difference between the two amounts will be amortized in future periods.

    c. Each period any necessary amortization reduces the investment account and appears on the income statement.

    d. Each period the investor company recognizes its percentage share of the investee's net income by increasing the asset account (Investment in Investee Company) by the appropriate amount and recognizing the amount as income for the period.

    e. Each period the investor recognizes the dividends received from the investee as dividend revenue on the income statement.

11-54. Which of the following statements is TRUE with respect to the consolidation of parent and subsidiary balance sheets?

    a. The parent's "Investment in Investee" account must be eliminated.

    b. If the parent paid any amount in excess of book value for the investment in the subsidiary, this amount must be set up in a separate asset account on the consolidated statements as "Excess of investment cost over equity acquired in net assets of Subsidiary."

    c. The subsidiary's paid-in capital and retained earnings must be eliminated;

    d. If the parent does not own 100% of the subsidiary, a "minority interest" account must be created for the portion not owned.

    e. All of the above statements are true.

CHAPTER TWELVE

POLICY MAKING

CHAPTER OUTLINE

MARKET ECONOMY

1. An economy is a system for allocating available resources to various uses.

2. In a centrally controlled system the national government directs virtually all uses of economic resources.

3. In a free market economy supply and demand in the marketplace determine prices for goods and services.

4. Most national economic systems fall somewhere between the two extremes. The U.S. economy tends toward a market system.

Capital formation in a market economy

1. The material standard of living of a society depends on how many goods and services can be produced in any period of time with the available resources.

2. In order for a high standard of living to be sustained, a high level of capital must be built up and maintained.

3. For capital formation to occur, some current consumption must be postponed.

4. Consumption is postponed through direct or indirect savings.

a. <u>Direct</u> saving takes place when an individual, family, or some other consumption unit does not spend all the funds it currently receives from its factors of production.

b. <u>Indirect</u> saving occurs when businesses distribute LESS than their current income as cash dividends to their owners.

5. Savings alone are not enough; the savings must be spent on new capital or replacements for capital used up in current production.

6. Balance is important.

a. An EXCESS of savings can lead to <u>unemployment</u>.

b. A LACK of savings leads to insufficient capital formation; then, demand for goods and services exceeds supply, leading to <u>inflation</u>.

7. To avoid serious unemployment or inflation there must be a systematic way to transfer funds from savers to those interested in using such funds.

8. The **capital market** consists of all the individuals and institutions that together accomplish the transfer of funds from savers to economic units that wish to spend additional funds on capital goods and services.

9. Financial intermediaries serve to link the interests of capital savers and capital users.

10. The segment of the capital market in which significant numbers of business enterprises raise funds is called the "markets for corporate securities".

Social demands on the corporate securities markets

1. For economic stability, the supply of funds must be matched against the demand for funds.

a. Firms often need to invest in capital goods that cost enormous amounts and last many years.

b. Savers usually want to invest relatively small amounts with

161

flexibility as to when they may recover the funds.

    c. Intermediaries balance saver and user needs.

2.   The **primary corporate securities market** consists of all transactions in which the money capital of business enterprises is expanded through the issue of new securities or reduced through the redemption, retirement, or liquidation of previously outstanding securities. (The trades directly involve the firm whose securities are being bought or sold.)

3.   The **secondary corporate securities market** consists of all trades of corporate securities **NOT** involving the business enterprise whose securities are bought or sold.

4.. Businesses must have access to enough funds at a low enough cost to ensure that they can replace worn-out capital and add new capital to the economy.

5.   For the market to generate a high level of investment opportunities between savers and users, the markets must be **operationally efficient**.

6.   A securities market is **operationally efficient** when all the intermediaries and others who participate in the transfer of funds from savers to users <u>earn no more than is necessary</u> to induce them to provide their services.

7.   Presumably, the best insurance against excessive fees for intermediaries is competition.

8.   In the absence of rigorous competition, there is a definite <u>social interest</u> in regulating the corporate securities markets intermediaries.

9.   For the market to generate a high level of investment opportunities between savers and users, the markets must be **reasonably fair.** This is the principal reason for regulation of corporate financial reporting.

<u>Role of financial accounting in corporate securities markets</u>

1.   Financial accounting information is used in a significant portion of the decisions made in corporate securities markets.

162

2. Financial accounting information is a critical link between savers and users of financial capital.

Principal-Agent relationship established

1. When investors entrust their capital to the managers of a business enterprise, a legally recognized and enforceable "agency" relationship is established.

2. As agents, managers have legal and ethical duties to render faithfully periodic reports about their activities.

Fairness of markets

1. When savers think that the markets are unfair (fraudulent, deceptive, and manipulative), the flow of new money capital shrinks.

2. High quality financial reporting contributes to fairness in financial markets.

3. The strength of accounting reports (and other items of financial information) has led many researchers in corporate finance to conclude that U.S. securities markets are **"efficient"** in the sense that securities prices quickly adjust to new information becoming available.

Public interest in financial reporting

1. If financial reporting from business managers is not fair, investors make wrong decisions. Capital misallocations will occur, and the markets will be unfair.

2. Unfair markets lead to excessive investment risks which, in turn, lead to capital withdrawal and/or capital flight.

FINANCIAL ACCOUNTING STANDARD SETTING

1. A history of abusive securities markets practices and deceptive financial reporting led to federal securities regulation.

2. The Securities Act of 1933

    a. requires adequate and accurate disclosure of material data
       - financial or otherwise
       - concerning securities to be sold in interstate commerce or
       - through the mail and

    b. specifically outlaws fraud in the sale of securities
       - whether or not newly issued
       - provides criminal penalties for offending parties, and
       - remedies for injured parties

    c. does NOT determine which firms are worthy of funds

    d. does NOT set the prices at which securities may be issued

    e. is mainly directed at the <u>primary</u> corporate securities market.

3. The Securities Exchange Act of 1934

    a. established the Securities and Exchange Commission (SEC)

    b. gave the SEC the authority to regulate
       - trading in securities
       - securities exchanges
       - the conduct and financial affairs of intermediaries
       - the accounting practices of business enterprises

    c. is mainly directed at the <u>secondary</u> corporate securities market.

4. Any business that wishes to have its securities traded on a national exchange must register with the SEC and file the reports required by the SEC.

5. Failure to file the required reports can result in suspension and/or withdrawal of the firm's securities from the exchange.

The process of financial accounting standards setting

1. The SEC has the power to prescribe accounting standards, but it has never done so directly.

2. The SEC chooses which accounting standards to enforce and retains absolute veto power over any and all such standards.

3. The development of accounting standards is left to the private sector.

4. Accounting standards are currently set by the Financial Accounting Standards Board (FASB).

5. The FASB is supported by a private foundation: the Financial Accounting Foundation (FAF).

6. The mission of the FASB is to establish and improve standards of financial accounting and reporting for the guidance and education of the public.

7. To accomplish its mission the FASB acts to:
    -   improve the usefulness of financial reporting
    -   keep standards current
    -   consider promptly any significant areas of deficiency
    -   improve the common understanding of the nature and purposes of information contained in financial reports.

8. The FASB develops its agenda through
    -   suggestions from interested parties
    -   an emerging issues task force
    -   an advisory council

9. The FASB sets standards through a lengthy "due process" which involves research, public discussion, exposure drafts, public hearings, and, finally, "Statements of Financial Accounting Standards (SFASs).

10. Standards which have been approved by the FASB and accepted by the SEC become binding on all financial statements and reports prepared in accordance with "generally accepted accounting principles" (GAAP).

11. GAAP are the total of all financial accounting standards, rules and regulations which must be observed in the preparation of financial reports acceptable to the SEC.

GOVERNMENTAL ACCOUNTING AND REPORTING

1. In the private sector the performance of an enterprise is judged by accounting income, which matches expenses to revenues.

2. Accounting income cannot be used to judge governmental agencies in the same way because
   - it is often difficult to define the products/services of governmental agencies,
   - there is no marketplace recognition of a service event (sales transaction),
   - it is difficult to measure the "economic worth" of a service event, and
   - "expenses" or outlays are typically "matched" to a governmental program rather than a product or service.

3. Since accounting profit cannot be used to evaluate government, there are three critical problems:
   - how to determine managerial performance,
   - how to compare the value of various governmental programs,
   - the relationship between costs and the public interest.

4. Governmental accounting has developed various procedures:
   - direct legislation usually creates a program,
   - the program is funded by legislative appropriations,
   - control over a program is exercised by comparing actual expenditures with appropriations.

5. Governmental accountability breaks down into three categories:
   - <u>fiscal accountability</u> involves appropriate spending of public funds in a lawful way with proper accounting;
   - <u>process accountability</u> requires that agencies carry out policies and programs in intended ways;
   - <u>program accountability</u> requires that governmental programs produce the results or changes intended.

6. Since 1985 governmental accounting standards have been set by the Governmental Accounting Standards Board (GASB), which, like the FASB, is under the control of the Financial Accounting Foundation.

7. Governmental accounting is much more diverse than business enterprise accounting, and prior to 1985 a number of competing groups issued standards.

8. The GASB does not have an enforcement agency (the role served by the SEC for the FASB), and many state and local governments do not always support the GASB's standards.

9. Standard setting for not-for-profit organizations is split between the FASB and the GASB. In 1989 accounting standards for public utilities, health care institutions and colleges and universities were assigned to the FASB. Standard setting for all remaining not-for-profit organizations is currently the responsibility of the GASB.

ACCOUNTING AS A SOCIAL FACTOR

1. Accounting concepts, standards, and procedures are created by people, and therefore, like law they are constantly changing.

2. Choices among accounting alternatives affect different firms in different ways; this leads to different distributions of wealth among various parties.

3. The question of which accounting policy is best is not determined by accounting theory; it is a matter of socioeconomic choice.

4. The choice of accounting policy is currently being made by the shared power system between the FASB and the SEC.

Historical cost measures

1. The fact that accounting policy decisions are social choices can be seen in the selection of historical cost as the measurement basis in U.S. accounting.

2. Prior to 1935 accounting differed greatly from company to company.

3. Given the ease with which it is understood and its objectivity, historical cost seems to fit the U.S. social spirit well.

Financial reporting format

1. Part of the social choice approach to financial accounting involves allowing a certain flexibility.

2. Ranges of "generally accepted accounting principles" are available.

3. Those preparing financial reports may choose among the available alternatives, but they must choose within the defined boundary lines.

4. Given the number of available accounting alternatives, the only way to

make the system work is to require firms to describe which choices they have made in elaborate notes to the financial statements.

5. Accounting practices cannot be explained by fundamental theories; such practices are _social_ choices.

6. One cannot prove that the U.S. financial reporting system is optimal; one can only observe that the U.S. financial reporting system appears to work well in our economy.

INTERNATIONAL ACCOUNTING

1. Given international economic interdependence, accounting must also be concerned with the global economy.

2. As accounting policy is a matter of social choice, and nations differ with respect to their social, economic, legal, and political systems, so accounting systems likewise differ.

3. Nations differ with respect to measurement and practices like consolidation.

4. Multinational corporations (MNCs) must integrate all of their national accounting systems and come up with single language/single currency financial statements.

5. The international market in corporate securities is huge.

6. Foreign companies wishing to sell securities in the U.S. must comply with SEC requirements. Thus, they must RESTATE their financial statements to U.S. GAAP, translate them into U.S dollars, and translate them into English.

7. Accounting across national borders creates technical problems such as the issues associated with foreign currency translation.

8. Many groups are involved in an effort to create international standards of accounting.

9. To date, the most effective group has been the International Federation of Accountants (IFAC), a group whose membership consists of national accounting organizations from more than seventy countries and which represents more than a million of the world's practicing professional accountants.

10. IFAC has two major standard setting committees, one for accounting and one for auditing. The International Accounting Standards Committee (IASC) has been at work since 1973 and had published 29 standards through the end of 1989.

11. International accounting standards are used by many MNCs when they report outside their home countries.

12. Many developing nations use international standards since this saves them from developing their own.

13. Progress in international accounting standard setting has been very slow.

14. One of the worst offenders is the U.S., which recognizes only domestic standards for purposes of reporting by U.S. corporations.

QUESTIONS AND EXERCISES

A. TRUE-FALSE. Indicate whether each of the following statements is true or false.

_____12-1. In a free market economy supply and demand in the marketplace determine prices for goods and services.

_____12-2. In order for a high standard of living to be sustained, a high level of capital must be built up and maintained.

_____12-3. Direct saving takes place when an individual, family, or some other consumption unit does not spend all the funds it currently receives from its factors of production.

_____12-4. Savings alone are enough to assure a high standard of living in a market economy.

_____12-5. A lack of savings can lead to inflation in a market economy.

_____ 12-6. The capital market consists of all the individuals and institutions that together accomplish the transfer of funds from savers to economic units that wish to spend additional funds on capital goods and services.

_____ 12-7. The market for corporate securities is that segment of the capital market in which significant numbers of individuals transfer their funds to banks.

_____ 12-8. Savers usually want to invest relatively small amounts with flexibility as to when they may recover the funds.

_____ 12-9. The role of intermediaries in the capital market is to keep savers from making bad investments.

_____ 12-10. The secondary corporate securities market consists of all trades of corporate securities NOT involving the business enterprise whose securities are bought or sold.

_____ 12-11. The primary corporate securities market consists of all trades of corporate securities NOT involving the business enterprise whose securities are bought or sold.

_____ 12-12. A securities market is operationally efficient when all the intermediaries and others who participate in the transfer of funds from saver to users earn no more than is necessary to induce them to provide their services.

_____ 12-13. A securities market is operationally efficient when all the intermediaries and others who participate in the transfer of funds from saver to users earn excessive profits in minimum time.

_____ 12-14. Regulation of the corporate securites markets cannot be justified in terms of the social interest.

_____ 12-15. The principal reason for regulation of corporate financial reporting is to assure that the markets are reasonably fair.

_____ 12-16. Financial accounting information is not often used in the decisions made in corporate securities markets.

_____ 12-17. Financial accounting information does not link savers and users of financial capital.

____12-18. The strength of accounting reports (and other items of financial information) has led many researchers in corporate finance to conclude that U.S. securities markets are "efficient" in the sense that securities prices quickly adjust to new information becoming available.

____12-19. If financial reporting from business managers is not fair, capital misallocations will occur, and the markets will be unfair.

____12-20. Unfair markets lead to capital withdrawal and/or capital flight.

____12-21. The Securities Act of 1933 requires adequate and accurate disclosure of material data (financial or otherwise) concerning securities to be sold in interstate commerce.

____12-22. The Securities Act of 1933 requires adequate and accurate disclosure of material financial (but not nonfinancial) data concerning securities to be sold in interstate commerce.

____12-23. The Securities Act of 1933 requires adequate and accurate disclosure of material data (financial or otherwise) concerning securities to be sold through the mail.

____12-24. The Securities Act of 1933 specifically outlaws fraud in the sale of securities (whether or not newly issued) but does not provide criminal penalties for offending parties, and remedies for injured parties.

____12-25. The Securities Act of 1933 provides remedies for those who have been injured by fraud in the sale of securities.

____12-26. The Securities Act of 1933 does not determine which firms are worthy of funds or set the prices at which securities may be issued.

____12-27. The Securities Act of 1933 is mainly directed at the primary corporate securities market.

____12-28. The Securities Exchange Act of 1934 established the Securities and Exchange Commission (SEC).

____12-29. The Securities Act of 1933 gave the SEC the authority to regulate trading in securities.

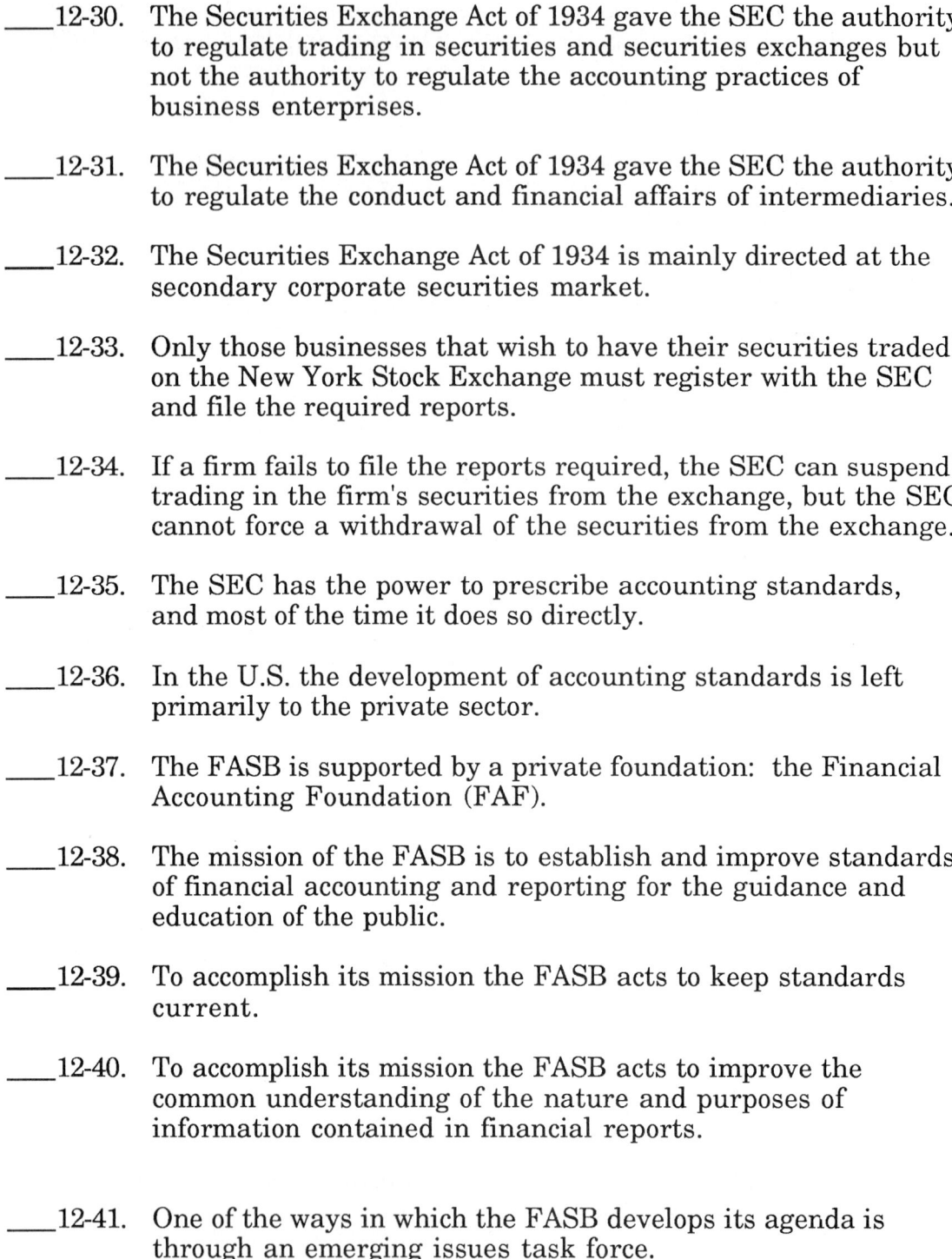

____12-30. The Securities Exchange Act of 1934 gave the SEC the authority to regulate trading in securities and securities exchanges but not the authority to regulate the accounting practices of business enterprises.

____12-31. The Securities Exchange Act of 1934 gave the SEC the authority to regulate the conduct and financial affairs of intermediaries.

____12-32. The Securities Exchange Act of 1934 is mainly directed at the secondary corporate securities market.

____12-33. Only those businesses that wish to have their securities traded on the New York Stock Exchange must register with the SEC and file the required reports.

____12-34. If a firm fails to file the reports required, the SEC can suspend trading in the firm's securities from the exchange, but the SEC cannot force a withdrawal of the securities from the exchange.

____12-35. The SEC has the power to prescribe accounting standards, and most of the time it does so directly.

____12-36. In the U.S. the development of accounting standards is left primarily to the private sector.

____12-37. The FASB is supported by a private foundation: the Financial Accounting Foundation (FAF).

____12-38. The mission of the FASB is to establish and improve standards of financial accounting and reporting for the guidance and education of the public.

____12-39. To accomplish its mission the FASB acts to keep standards current.

____12-40. To accomplish its mission the FASB acts to improve the common understanding of the nature and purposes of information contained in financial reports.

____12-41. One of the ways in which the FASB develops its agenda is through an emerging issues task force.

_____12-42. Standards which have been approved by the FASB and accepted by the SEC become binding on all financial statements and reports prepared in accordance with "generally accepted accounting principles" (GAAP).

_____12-43. Accounting income cannot be used to judge governmental agencies in the same way as it is used in the private sector because, among other things, it is often difficult to define the products/services of governmental agencies.

_____12-44. In governmental accounting "expenses" or outlays are typically "matched" to a governmental program rather than a product or service.

_____12-45. In governmental accounting control over a program is typically exercised by comparing actual expenditures with appropriations.

_____12-46. Process accountability requires that governmental programs produce the results or changes intended.

_____12-47. Since 1985 governmental accounting standards have been set by the Governmental Accounting Standards Board (GASB), which, like the FASB, is under the control of the Financial Accounting Foundation.

_____12-48. Prior to 1985 a number of competing groups issued governmental accounting standards.

_____12-49. State and local governments always support the GASB's standards.

_____12-50. In 1989 accounting standards for public utilities, health care institutions and colleges and universities were assigned to the FASB.

_____12-51. Choices among accounting alternatives affect different firms in different ways; but this has no effect on distributions of wealth among various parties.

_____12-52. The question of which accounting policy is best is a matter of socioeconomic choice.

_____12-53. Given the ease with which it is understood and its objectivity, historical cost seems to fit the U.S. social spirit well.

____12-54. Given the number of available accounting alternatives, the only way to make the system work is to require firms to describe which choices they have made in elaborate notes to the financial statements.

____12-55. Nations differ with respect to accounting measurement and practices like consolidation.

____12-56. To date, the most effective group involved in the effort to create international standards of accounting has been the International Federation of Accountants (IFAC).

____12-57. Many developing nations use international standards.

____12-58. The SEC probably represents the greatest single influence upon the financial information of large corporations that reaches the public.

____12-59. The Financial Accounting Standards Board has ultimate jurisdiction over financial accounting measurements and disclosures made by firms whose stock is traded on U.S. stock exchanges.

____12-60. One of the advantages of accounting is that it does not change much from nation to nation.

CHAPTER THIRTEEN

FINANCIAL REPORTING AND ANALYSIS

CHAPTER OUTLINE

FINANCIAL REPORTING

1. Financial reporting is broader than financial statement preparation.

2. Financial reports contain complete or abbreviated financial statements.

3. Financial reports also contain other descriptions, explanations, and analyses.

4. Examples of financial reports include: corporate annual reports, various filings with regulatory commissions, and registration statements.

5. Financial reporting is useful to: economic policy makers, government regulators, parties making economic decisions affecting their own relationships with an entity, and entities seeking funds from others.

Types of Financial Reports

1. **Annual corporate reports**

    a. These may be required by
        i.   the state law governing the corporation and/or by
        ii. the exchange on which the stock is traded.

b. Components of an annual report include:
    i. Report of management-in which management
        - Takes responsibility for the integrity and objectivity of the financial information
        - Discusses internal control, adherence to company policy, and so forth
        - Gives assurance as to the reliability of the information system and the report
    ii. Report of independent accountants
        - Audit report- described in Chapter 14.
    iii. Primary financial statements
        - Consolidated Statement of Financial Position
        - Consolidated Statement of Income
        - Consolidated Statement of Cash Flows
    iv. Management discussion and analysis of results of operations and financial condition - includes
        - important unusual events and uncertainties
        - financial trends
        - the effects of new products or new services
        - significant past or anticipated changes in liquidity
        - the overall status of capital resources
    v. Secondary financial statements (e.g., statement of stockholders' equity)
    vi. Notes to financial statements -explain
        - significant accounting policies utilized
        - extent of involvement in multinational business
        - effects of specific financial accounting measurement policies selected by management
        - taxation
        - segments of business
    vii. Ten-year comparison of selected financial data
    viii. Selected quarterly data
    ix. Supplemental financial information - covers items such as
        - stock prices;
        - costs/benefits of environmental protection efforts;
        - numbers of employees at different plants and locations, and so forth.

2. **Summary annual reports**

a. Since 1987 the SEC has permitted companies to issue annual reports in whatever form they wish as long as they continue to file all required financial information with the SEC.

b. A number of companies have begun to issue condensed reports to stockholders.

3. **Quarterly financial reports**

   a. Required of most companies listed on public exchanges

   b. May have additional measurement problems due to such things as seasonalities

   c. Are generally considered less reliable than annual reports

   d. Can be useful in predicting the future cash-generating ability of the business

4. **SEC reporting**

   a. Requires that annual reports be issued to external parties

   b. Requires that audited annual reports be filed with the SEC

      i. referred to as 10-Ks
      ii. include more detail than a typical report to external parties
      iii. may be obtained from companies, the SEC, commercial services, etc.

   c. Requires extensive disclosure and a prospectus from firms planning to issue new stocks

   d. Requires (unaudited) quarterly financial reports (10-Qs)

5. **News announcements**

   a. SEC requires that large, publicly traded firms release certain financial information to the press as soon as it is measured.

   b. Typically, sales and earnings for the quarter or the year must be announced.

   c. Such announcements are timely because they generally are available at least 30 days prior to the release of the annual or interim reports.

6. **Financial services**

    a. Commercial services provide reports which generally include more detail than news announcements but less than that found in quarterly and annual reports.

    b. Include companies such as: Moody's, Standard & Poor's and Value Line, and so forth.

FINANCIAL ANALYSIS

Investment Decision Perspective

1. The investment decision problem is used to illustrate the decision relevance of information from financial reports.

2. The first task is specifying future cash flows (expected return).

3. In addition one must assess the risk associated with the cash flows (expected risk).

Estimating Investment Decision Factors from Financial Report Information

1. The estimation depends upon the assumption that historical data are relevant to future expectations.

2. The meaning and significance of the dollar values in financial reports depend on an understanding of

    a. the business environment which the numbers represent;

    b. the relationship of the numbers to the underlying economic transactions and events that are the real items of interest;

    c. the relationship of any particular number or set of numbers to other numbers included in the report;

    d. the relationships of the figures to previous years' performance and to performance of similar companies.

3. Two important requirements for interpretation are scaling and standards.

    a. Scaling is the process of relating one number to another

number (ratios).

  b. The investor is interested in the relationship between numbers and some <u>standard</u>.

    i. <u>Time standards</u>

      a. These use numbers (or ratios) from preceding time periods so that the investor can assess the progress of the firm in relation to prior performance

      b. Present accounting policy requires the inclusion of data both from the most recently ended accounting period and from the preceding period in financial reports.

    ii. <u>Industry standards</u>

      a. Use the performance of other business enterprises for comparison.

      b. Can be based either on the performance of all other corporations or only on the performance of firms in the same industry.

      c. Are available from commercial financial services.

Statistical Measures

There are a number of indicators that are commonly used as a basis for estimating risk and return.

Indicators of Return

1. Earnings per share (EPS)

  a. EPS is the earnings attributable to each share of common stock.

  b. If the company has preferred stock, the dividend requirements must be deducted from net income.

  c. If the preferred stock is participating, this must be taken into account.

  d. If there are any convertible instruments in the firm's

capital structure (stock options, or bonds and/or preferred stock that are convertible to common stock), the number of shares outstanding could be affected by conversion of any such securities.

i. If, at the date of issuance, the convertible security is determined to derive a "significant" portion of its market value from the conversion feature, it is considered a "common stock equivalent"

the number of shares that would be issued at conversion of such "common stock equivalents" are added to the common shares actually outstanding to derive the EPS figure;

this figure is referred to as "primary earnings per share"

Primary Earnings Per Share $=$ $\dfrac{\text{Net income - preferred dividends}}{\substack{\text{Number of shares of common stock outstanding} \\ + \text{ Number of shares represented by common stock} \\ \text{equivalents}}}$

ii. If, at date of issuance, the convertible security is NOT a common stock equivalent,

then the potentially issuable common shares are not included in the calculation of primary earnings per share.

However, as these securities MAY be converted, they are used in the calculation of "fully diluted earnings per share".

All the outstanding convertible securities are assumed to be converted into common stock, and the number of shares that would be issued is added to the common shares outstanding used in the denominator of the EPS ratio.

Fully diluted Earnings Per Share $=$ $\dfrac{\text{Net income - preferred dividends}}{\substack{\text{Number of shares of common stock outstanding} \\ + \text{ Number of shares represented by common stock} \\ \text{equivalents} + \text{Number of shares represented by} \\ \text{all remaining convertible securities}}}$

2. Earnings yield

This measure relates EPS more directly to expected return.

$$\text{Earnings yield} = \frac{\text{EPS - Cash dividend per share}}{\text{Average annual price per share}}$$

3. Net Income to Owners' Equity and/or Assets

a. These are measures of the efficiency with which capital is used by the firm.

b. They are computed by dividing the measure of return (the net income) by an investment base.

c. Since the purpose is to show the efficiency of capital utilized during the period, the AVERAGE levels of total assets or owners' equity are used.

e. **Return on Assets** $= \dfrac{\text{Net Income + Interest Expense}}{\text{Average total assets}}$

   i. Since the investment base used is total assets (both those financed by owners and those financed by creditors), the measure should NOT include the cost of the various types of financing; thus, interest expense is added back to net income to eliminate this cost.

   ii. This measure is important in assessing the performance of two of more companies having different mixes of debt and owners' equity.

d. **Return on Owners' Equity** $= \dfrac{\text{Net Income}}{\text{Average Owners' Equity}}$

   i. Investors are also interested in the return to them as holders of common stock.

   ii. In this case the denominator is owners' equity, also

called "net assets" (only those assets financed by owners).

  iii. This measure reflects the scaled return accruing to shareholders on their equity.

  iv. It is larger than the return on assets because the return on total assets (net income) is larger than the cost of (interest paid on) all the liabilities; this is known as the <u>leverage effect.</u>

4. <u>Net Income to Sales (Revenues)</u>

  a. This ratio indicates the amount of profit that is generated from each dollar of sales.

  b. **Net income to sales** $= \dfrac{\text{Net income}}{\text{Sales and revenues}}$

  c. Whether a particular return for a dollar of revenue is good or bad depends on

  i. the total volume of revenue that a firm generates

  ii. the investment required to generate this level of revenue.

  d. The net-income-to-revenue statistic is related to the return on investment by owners as follows:

  Return on Owners' Equity $= \dfrac{\text{Net Income}}{\text{Sales and Revenues}} \times \dfrac{\text{Sales and revenues}}{\text{Average Owners' Equity}}$

  i. The sales and revenues ÷ average owners' equity indicates the number of times that the total owners' investment "turns over" during the year.

  ii. For firms that turn over total investment frequently, a lower profit per dollar of sales can be sustained while generating a reasonably good return on total investment.

  iii. Similarly, a firm that has a slow turnover of investment may require a higher return on each dollar of revenue in order to maintain a similar return on investment.

Indicators of Risk

1. Current and acid-test ratios

    a. Are indicators of a company's short-term solvency (the ability to pay bills when due).

    b. **Current ratio** $= \dfrac{\text{Current assets}}{\text{Current liabilities}}$

        i. This ratio indicates how many dollars of current assets are available to "back up" each dollar of current liabilities.

        ii. The larger the current ratio the less the risk of default and bankruptcy.

        iii. The current assets in the numerator of the current ratio include the value of inventories; inventories are not readily available for settlement of liabilities.

    c. **Acid-test ratio** $= \dfrac{\text{Quick assets}}{\text{Current liabilities}}$

        i. This is a more stringent indicator of short-term solvency.

        ii. "Quick assets" are those which are fairly quickly convertible into cash; they include: cash, marketable securities, and accounts receivable.

        iii. This ratio indicates how many dollars of quick assets are available to "back up" each dollar of current liabilities

2. Debt-Equity Ratio

    a. **Debt-equity ratio** $= \dfrac{\text{Total liabilities}}{\text{Total liabilities and owners' equity}}$

    b. This ratio indicates the percentage of funds provided by creditors.

    c. The higher the percentage of creditor financing, the

riskier the investment is in terms of solvency.

d. The higher the percentage of creditor financing the potentially larger the return that might accrue to the owners (in good times) from the leverage effect.

e. A similar measure that focuses on the firm's long-term capitalization would use only the <u>long-term</u> liabilities in the numerator.

3. <u>Times interest earned</u>

a. This indicates the extent to which interest requirements are covered by net income.

b. The greater the number of times interest earned the smaller the possibility that the firm will be unable to make interest payments when due.

c. The measure utilizes income before interest and income tax expenses since that is the amount available to pay interest obligations.

d. **Times Interest Earned** $= \dfrac{\text{Before tax income + interest expense}}{\text{Interest expense}}$

4. <u>Some limitations of financial ratios.</u>

a. The interpretation of any single statistic is based upon the assumption that all other measures remain constant.

b. In fact, whether a higher or lower value is desirable for any single statistic is a function of the values for all related financial statistics and all other sources of information about the enterprise.

c. Accounting measurement policies result in limitations of the usefulness of ratios.

   i. Current market values (rather than historical costs) may relate better to the intended information of a particular ratio.

   ii. The dollars of various original transaction amounts

(established at various times in the past) do not represent the same economic sacrifice as time passes and the general level of prices changes.

THE COMPARABILITY QUESTION

Comparability Over Time

1. To enhance comparability over time, present accounting policy includes the consistency principle

2. This principle urges use of the same accounting policies by a given firm from one time period to the next.

3. When an accounting policy is changed, the consistency principle calls for prominent disclosure of the change and its dollar impact.

Comparability Between Firms

1. Different firms in different industries, and in many cases within the same industry, use different accounting methods.

2. At present the trade-off between the advantages and disadvantages of uniformity and flexibility has been resolved in favor of substantial flexibility for management.

Enhancing Comparability Between Firms

1. "Full disclosure" of all important facts has long been a financial reporting rule and a legal requirement embodied in the securities acts of 1933 and 1934.

2. The FASB and the SEC have increasingly broadened the interpretation of what constitutes important relevant information.

3. The investor now receives a large amount of supplementary information which may be helpful in reconciling differences in accounting methods between firms.

4. There is considerable consensus that the number of acceptable accounting alternatives should be reduced.

5. As long as management continues to have some flexibility in

choosing the accounting policies to be used in preparing financial reports, it seems reasonable that investors will want some type of independent review (audit) of management's choices.

QUESTIONS AND EXERCISES

_____13-1. Financial reporting is narrower than financial statement preparation.

_____13-2. Financial reports can contain abbreviated financial statements.

_____13-3. Financial reporting is useful only to investors and creditors.

_____13-4. Annual corporate reports may be required only by the state law governing the corporation.

_____13-5. In the management report company management states that the auditor is responsible for the objectivity of the financial information.

_____13-6. The set of primary financial statements includes: the Consolidated Statement of Financial Position, the Consolidated Statement of Income, and the Consolidated Statement of Changes in Stockholder Equities.

_____13-7. The management discussion and analysis of results of operations and financial condition includes: discussion (among other items) of the effects of new products or new services and of the overall status of capital resources.

_____13-8. An annual report includes only: the report of management, the report of the independent auditors, the primary financial statements, and the notes to the statements.

_____13-9. The notes to financial statements explain any significant accounting policies utilized by the company.

____13-10. Supplemental financial information covers items such as stock prices, costs and benefits of environmental protection efforts, the numbers of employees at different plants and locations, and so forth.

____13-11. Companies may issue condensed reports to stockholders, if they prefer not to issue complete reports.

____13-12. Quarterly financial reports are required of most companies listed on public exchanges

____13-13. Quarterly financial reports have only the measurement problems that arise with annual reports.

____13-14. Quarterly reports are generally considered more reliable than annual reports because they cover a shorter time period.

____13-15. Quarterly reports can be useful in predicting the future cash-generating ability of a business.

____13-16. SEC reporting requires annual reports to external parties.

____13-17. SEC reporting requires annual reports be filed with the Commission, but these need not be audited.

____13-18. The reports filed with the SEC (10-Ks) include less detail than a typical report to external parties.

____13-19. The SEC requires extensive disclosure and a prospectus from firms planning to manufacture new products.

____13-20. The SEC does not require such news releases, but large, publicly traded firms voluntarily release certain financial information to the press as soon as it is measured.

____13-21. Commercial financial services provide reports which generally include more detail than news announcements but less than that found in quarterly and annual reports.

____13-22. The first task in an investment decision problem is specifying future cash flows (expected return).

____13-23. Estimating investment decision factors from financial report information depends upon the assumption that historical data are relevant to future expectations.

____13-24. The meaning and significance of the dollar values in financial reports depend on an understanding of the relationships of the figures to previous years' performance and to performance of similar companies.

____13-25. Scaling is an important requirement for interpretation of financial reports.

____13-26. Standards are the process of relating one number to another number (ratios).

____13-27. Time standards use numbers (or ratios) from preceding time periods so that the investor can assess the progress of the firm in relation to prior performance.

____13-28. Present accounting policy requires the inclusion of data from the preceding period in corporate financial reports.

____13-29. Indicators of return include: earnings per share, earnings yield, income to owners' equity, income to assets, and times interest earned.

____13-30. If there are any convertible instruments in the firm's capital structure (stock options, or bonds and/or preferred stock that are convertible to common stock), the number of shares outstanding could be affected by conversion of any such securities.

____13-31. If, at the date of issuance, a convertible security is determined to derive a "significant" portion of its market value from the conversion feature, it is considered a "common stock equivalent".

____13-32. Only the fully diluted earnings per share figure takes into account the number of shares represented by common stock equivalents.

____13-33. The fully diluted earnings per share figure takes into account both the number of shares represented by common stock equivalents and the number of shares represented by all remaining convertible securities.

____13-34. Return on assets and return on equity are computed by dividing the measure of return (the net income) by an investment base.

____13-35. In calculating the return on assets, since the investment base used is total assets (both those financed by owners and those financed by creditors), the measure should NOT include the cost of the various types of financing; thus, interest expense is added back to net income to eliminate this cost.

____13-36. Return on assets is an important measure in assessing the performance of two or more companies having different mixes of debt and owners' equity.

____13-37. Return on owners' equity reflects the scaled return accruing to creditors.

____13-38. Return on owners' equity is smaller than the return on assets because the return on total assets (net income) is larger than the cost of (interest paid on) all the liabilities; this is known as the leverage effect.

____13-39. Whether a particular return for a dollar of revenue is good or bad depends on the total volume of revenue that a firm generates.

____13-40. Whether a particular return for a dollar of revenue is good or bad depends on the investment required to generate this level of revenue.

____13-41. A firm that has a slow turnover of investment may require a higher return on each dollar of revenue in order to maintain a return on investment similar to firms with higher turnovers.

____13-42. The current and acid-test ratios are indicators of a company's short-term solvency (the ability to pay bills when due).

____13-43. The current ratio indicates how many dollars of current liabilities are available to "back up" each dollar of current assets.

____13-44. The smaller the current ratio the less the risk of default and bankruptcy.

____13-45. The current assets in the numerator of the current ratio include the value of accounts receivable which are not readily available for settlement of liabilities.

____13-46. The acid-test ratio is a less stringent indicator of short-term solvency than the current ratio.

____13-47. "Quick assets" are those which are fairly quickly convertible into cash. These include: cash, marketable securities, accounts receivable, and inventories.

____13-48. The debt-equity ratio indicates the percentage of funds provided by owners.

____13-49. The higher the percentage of owner financing, the riskier the investment is in terms of solvency.

____13-50. The higher the percentage of owner financing the potentially larger the return that might accrue to the owners (in good times) from the leverage effect.

____13-51. The times interest earned measure indicates the extent to which interest requirements are covered by sales.

____13-52. The greater the number of times interest earned the larger the possibility that the firm will be unable to make interest payments when due.

____13-53. The times interest earned measure utilizes income after interest and income tax expenses since that is the amount available to pay interest obligations.

____13-54. The interpretation of any single statistic is based upon the assumption that all other measures remain constant.

____13-55. Whether a higher or lower value is desirable for any single statistic is a function of the values for all related financial statistics and all other sources of information about the enterprise.

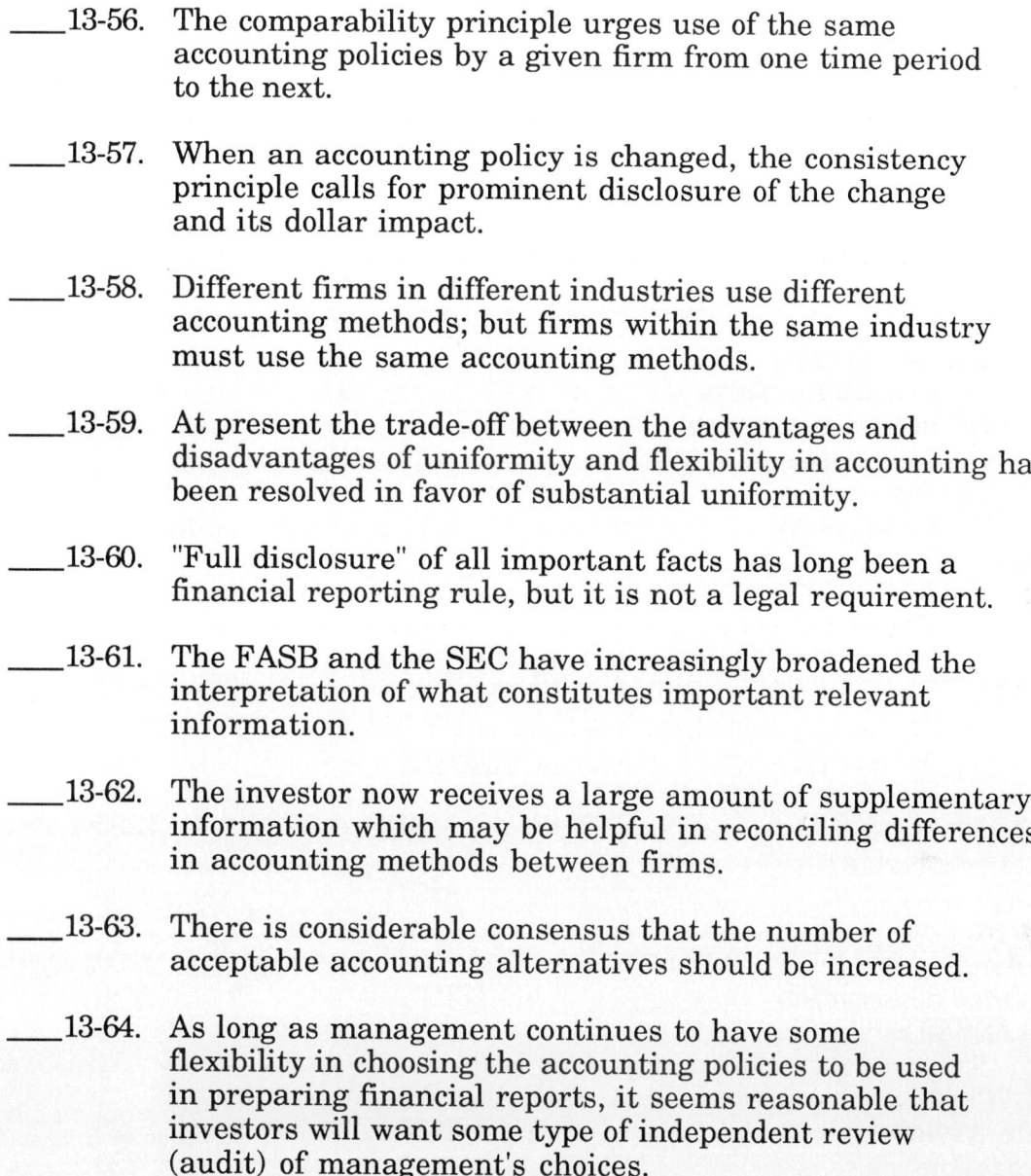

____13-56. The comparability principle urges use of the same accounting policies by a given firm from one time period to the next.

____13-57. When an accounting policy is changed, the consistency principle calls for prominent disclosure of the change and its dollar impact.

____13-58. Different firms in different industries use different accounting methods; but firms within the same industry must use the same accounting methods.

____13-59. At present the trade-off between the advantages and disadvantages of uniformity and flexibility in accounting has been resolved in favor of substantial uniformity.

____13-60. "Full disclosure" of all important facts has long been a financial reporting rule, but it is not a legal requirement.

____13-61. The FASB and the SEC have increasingly broadened the interpretation of what constitutes important relevant information.

____13-62. The investor now receives a large amount of supplementary information which may be helpful in reconciling differences in accounting methods between firms.

____13-63. There is considerable consensus that the number of acceptable accounting alternatives should be increased.

____13-64. As long as management continues to have some flexibility in choosing the accounting policies to be used in preparing financial reports, it seems reasonable that investors will want some type of independent review (audit) of management's choices.

B. MULTIPLE CHOICE. Select the best response to each of the following, and mark the letter corresponding to your choice.

Belved Company had 500 common shares outstanding throughout 19X7.

Belved Company
Income Statement
For 19X7

Sales revenue		$480
Cost of goods sold	90	
Wages expense	90	
Advertising expense	30	
Depreciation expense	80	
Rent expense	15	
Interest expense	8	
Total expenses		($313)
Net Income		$167

Belved Company
Balance Sheets

	12/31/X6	12/31/X7
ASSETS		
Cash	$150	$290
Accounts receivable	$100	$200
Inventory	$250	$230
Prepaid rent	$20	$15
Equipment	$600	$700
Accumulated depreciation	($150)	($230)
TOTAL ASSETS	$970	$1,205
LIABILITIES		
Accounts payable	$175	$125
Wages payable	$0	$20
Interest payable	$10	$8
Mortgage payable	$300	$250
OWNERS' EQUITY (OE)		
Paid-in Capital	$485	$685
Retained earnings	$0	$117
TOTAL LIABILITIES AND OE	$970	$1,205

Use the information for Belved Company for the next eight questions.

13-65. Belved Company's earnings per share for 19X7 was:

    a. $.334
    b. $.234
    c. $.10
    d. None of the above.

13-66. Belved Company's return on assets (to the nearest tenth) for 19X7 was:

    a.   16.1%
    b.   15.4%
    c.   14.5%
    d.   13.9%

13-67. Belved Company's return on equity (to the nearest tenth) for 19X7 was:

    a.   26.0%
    b.   20.1%
    c.   21.8%
    d. None of the above.

13-68. Belved Company's net income to sales (to the nearest tenth) for 19X7 was:

    a.   34.2%
    b.   36.5%
    c.   34.8%
    d. None of the above.

13-69. Belved Company's current ratio (to the nearest tenth) at December 31, 19X7 was:

    a. 3.2 : 1
    b. 3.3 : 1
    c. 4.7 : 1
    d. 4.8 : 1

13-70. Belved Company's acid-test ratio (to the nearest tenth) at December 31, 19X7 was:

    a. 3.2 : 1
    b. 3.3 : 1
    c. 4.7 : 1
    d. 4.8 : 1

13-71. Belved Company's debt-equity ratio (to the nearest tenth) at December 31, 19X7 was:

    a. 12.7%
    b. 33.4%
    c. 20.7%
    d. None of the above.

13-72. Belved Company's times interest earned (to the nearest tenth) for 19X7 was:

    a. 21.9
    b. 20.9
    c. 19.9
    d. None of the above.

CHAPTER FOURTEEN

AUDITING

CHAPTER OUTLINE

1. The focus shifts from quantity and types of information to quality of information.

2. The U.S. accounting profession has been growing at a much faster rate than the population of the U.S.

3. A U.S. Bureau of Labor Statistics's study estimated that demand for accountants will increase 40 percent during the 1990s.

The CPA Profession

1. CPA certificates and state licenses to practice are issued by the individual states and territories.

2. Prerequisites for a CPA certificate typically include:
   - a degree from an accredited college/university
   - passing the CPA exam
   - practical experience under the supervision of a CPA
   - knowledge of local professional ethics statutes
   - satisfactory personal references.

3. The American Institute of CPAs (AICPA)
   - acts as the profession's advocate
   - establishes guidelines and "generally accepted auditing standards"
   - prepares and administers the CPA exam twice a year.

4. State Societies of CPAs are concerned with local/regional matters.

Role of Auditing

1. Audits allow user groups to use financial statements with confidence.

2. Audits do NOT guarantee the accuracy of financial statements; they provide reasonable assurance that the statements "fairly present" the financial situation of the company.

3. Management is responsible for the financial statements; the auditor adds credibility to management's financial statements.

Audit reports

1. The standard "**unqualified**" ("clean") audit report

   - is used when an examination reveals no reservations about the adequacy of the financial statements under audit;
   - is addressed to the board of directors and the shareholders of the company whose financial statements have been examined;
   - is dated and signed;
   - is presented in three paragraphs.

   - **Paragraph one**
     - names the company and items audited
     - points out that the financial statements are the responsibility of company's management
     - indicates that the auditor's job is to express an opinion

   - **Paragraph two**
     - states that the audit was conducted in accordance with GAAS (generally accepted auditing standards);
     - indicates that GAAS require that the audit obtain reasonable assurance as to whether the financial statements are free of material misstatement;
     - states that an audit includes examining, on a test basis, evidence supporting principles used and significant estimates made by management;
     - states that the auditors believe that the audit provides a reasonable basis for the opinion.

- **Paragraph three**
  - indicates that the financial statements
    - "present fairly",
    - in all material respects
      - the financial position of the firm
      - the results of its operations
      - and its cash flows
    - in conformity with GAAP

2. **"Qualified" opinions** are issued
   - when the <u>scope</u> of an examination has been <u>limited</u>;
   - when there is <u>disagreement</u> with one or more aspects of the financial statements;
   - when an <u>inherent uncertainty</u> exists.

   - **Paragraphs one and two are the same** as above.

   - **Paragraph three would modify the opinion**, stating that <u>"except for"</u> or <u>"subject to"</u> certain circumstances the financial statements "present fairly" in conformity with GAAP.

   - **A fourth paragraph is added** to explain the circumstances of the qualification.

3. **"Adverse" opinions** are issued if the financial statements do NOT "present fairly" the financial position, results of operations and cash flows of a company.

4. A **"disclaimer"** of an opinion is given
   - when the auditor has not been able to obtain sufficient evidence or
   - the financial statements are fundamentally impacted by uncertainty (e.g., a high probability of bankruptcy).

Responsibility for financial statements

1. The auditor is solely responsible for the audit report.

2. Management is responsible for the financial statements.

3. It is management's responsibility to
   - adopt sound accounting policies,
   - maintain adequate and effective systems of accounts,
   - safeguard enterprise assets,
   - devise control systems to accomplish these goals.

Effects of independent audits

1. Audits can produce "report card" effects (people do their jobs better/more carefully because the auditors are/will be present).

2. Auditing may prevent some employee fraud.

3. Knowing that independent audit procedures will eventually test their financial representations, managements are probably less prone to make deliberately or intentionally biased judgments and estimates than would otherwise be the case.

Efficiency provided by independent audits

1. Users of financial information want assurances about its validity and reliability.

2. If each user had to obtain such assurance individually, the process would be immensely costly.

3. Research by Professor Wallace indicates that "economic incentives exist for parties to have and to supply an audit".

4. According to Wallace the audit fulfills three specific demands:

   - demand for a monitoring mechanism,
   - demand for information production to improve investors' decisions,
   - demand for insurance to protect against losses from distorted information.

Importance of internal control

1. Until the late 1940s auditing was viewed primarily as a process of "auditing the books" (examining documents supporting the transactions and verifying classification).

2. In 1949 auditors began to place greater reliance on internal control considerations.

3. "Internal control comprises the plan of organization and all of the coordinated methods and measures adopted within a business to safeguard its assets, check the accuracy and reliability of accounting data, promote operational efficiency, and encourage adherence to prescribed managerial principles."

4. If a company's internal controls operate well, the system is likely to produce reasonably complete and accurate financial data; as a consequence, audit tests can be reduced.

Auditing framework

1. At the beginning of an audit the auditor assumes
   - the internal control system is appropriate and effective,
   - GAAP have been applied in all processes underlying the financial statements,
   - the GAAP utilized have been applied consistently between the current and the prior periods,
   - there is adequate disclosure in the financial statements and the footnotes.

2. The auditor then gathers evidence to enable the confirmation or rejection of these assumptions.

3. The major steps of the audit are

   - become acquainted with the firm,
   - review and evaluate the management and the accounting control system in operation,
   - gather evidence on the integrity of the system,
   - gather evidence related to the representations made in the financial statements,
   - formulate an opinion.

4. Evidence is obtained by tests, selected observations, and statistical sampling.

5. The audit opinion is based on professional judgment.

6. Auditing standards differ from procedures. "Procedures" relates to acts to be performed; "standards" deal with measures of the quality of the performance of those acts and the objectives to be attained by the use of the procedures.

7. **Generally accepted auditing standards (GAAS)** include

   a. Three general standards
      i. The audit is to be performed by a person or persons having <u>adequate</u> technical <u>training and proficiency</u> as an auditor.
      ii. In all matters relating to the assignment, an <u>independence</u> in mental attitude is to be maintained by the auditor or auditors.
      iii. <u>Due professional care</u> is to be exercised in the performance of the audit and the preparation of the report.

   b. Three standards of field work
      i. The work is to be <u>adequately planned</u> and assistants, if any, are to be <u>properly supervised</u>.
      ii. A sufficient understanding of the <u>internal control</u> structure is to be obtained to plan the audit and to determine the nature, timing, and extent of tests to be performed.
      iii. Sufficient competent <u>evidential mattter</u> is to be obtained through inspection, observation, inquiries, and confirmation to afford a reasonable basis for an opinion regarding the financial statements under audit.

   c. Four standards of reporting
      i. The report shall state whether the financial statements are prepared <u>in accordance with generally accepted accounting principles</u>.
      ii. The report shall identify those circumstances in which such principles have <u>not been consistently observed</u> in the current period in relation to the preceding period.
      iii. Informative <u>disclosure</u> in the financial statements is to be regarded as <u>reasonably adequate</u> unless otherwise stated in the report.
      iv. The report shall either contain an <u>expression of opinion</u> regarding the financial statements, taken as a whole, or an assertion to the effect that an opinion cannot be expressed, the reasons therefore should be stated.

      In all cases where an auditor's name is associated with financial statements, the report should contain a clear-cut indication of the character of the auditor's work and the degree of responsibility the auditor is taking.

8. These generally accepted auditing standards are binding on CPAs.

   - CPAs who are member of the AICPA are required to observe its Professional Code of Conduct.

   - State CPA licensing requirements sometimes build the auditing standards into a state accountancy statute.

   - Administrative agencies like the SEC enforce the standards.

9. Note that the CPA profession itself SETS the standards.

10. Auditing procedures are less clearly established than GAAS. They are much more dependent on professional judgments, as no two companies or transactions are completely alike.

11. GAAS are determined by the AICPA. They are issued in formal pronouncements called "Statements on Auditing Standards" (SAS).

12. The International Auditing Practices Committee (IAPC), a senior committee of the International Federation of Accountants (IFAC), sets and publishes International Auditing Guidelines (IAGs).

13. IAGs do not override local regulations, but are intended for global acceptance.

An audit engagement

1. Audits are initiated due to

   - SEC requirements,
   - referrals by head offices of companies or home offices of large, international CPA firms,
   - suggestions from attorneys, bankers, or other business persons.

2. Planning procedures include staff assignments, establishing dates for the auditors' visits, determining necessary documents and information, and so forth.

3. The primary goal of the independent auditors is to express an opinion on the fairness of the representations in the financial statements.

4. The tests and other necessary procedures that are included in an audit are documented in a set of audit working papers. The AICPA recommends that the **working papers show**:

   a. data sufficient to demonstrate that the financial statements or other information upon which the auditor is reporting are in agreement with (or reconciled with) the client's record;

   b. that the engagement has been planned and that the work of any assistants was supervised and reviewed;

   c. that the client's system of internal control was reviewed and evaluated in determining necessary audit tests;

   d. the auditing procedures followed and tests performed in obtaining evidence;

   e. how exceptions and unusual matters were resolved or treated;

   f. comments indicating the auditors' conclusions about significant aspects of the engagement.

Special auditing tools and techniques

1. Statistical sampling can be applied where the sets of documents constituting evidential matter are relatively large and homogeneous.

2. Computer-assisted auditing procedures are also used in the audit process.

Detection of errors and irregularities (including fraud)

1. An audit made in accordance with GAAS includes <u>reasonable procedures</u> designed to detect material errors or irregularities.

2. SAS No. 53 requires
   - the audit design to provide reasonable assurance of detecting errors and irregularities that are material
   - the communication of all consequential errors and irregularities to the client's audit committee.

Professional independence

1. Independence is the cornerstone of the auditing profession.

2. Public confidence in independent auditors' reports would be impaired if there were evidence that independence was <u>actually</u> lacking.

3. Confidence may also be impaired by a lack of independence in <u>appearance.</u>

4. The auditor must be free from any obligation or interest in the client, its management or owners:

5. Outside auditors cannot own any stock in the companies they audit.

6. The AICPA's Code of Professional Conduct requires that CPAs acting as independent auditors must avoid situations that may lead outsiders to doubt their independence.

7. Since managements often directly pay auditors' fees, an economic relationship necessarily exists between the auditor and the auditee.

8. The creation of audit committees among corporate boards of directors as the boards' conduits to their independent auditors has alleviated but not eliminated this economic dilemma.

9. Board audit committees typically are comprised of outside directors (not corporate officers or employees).

10. Board audit committees
-monitor management activities,
-periodically review all corporate internal control procedures,
-receive reports from internal auditors, and
-serve as primary liaison with independent auditors.

11. The New York Stock Exchange (NYSE) requires that all companies whose securities are listed on the NYSE have audit committees consisting of outside board members.

12. The SEC and AICPA strongly recommend audit committees.

13. Mental attitudes are difficult to change through laws and codes of conduct. Despite all outward appearances of independence, the behavioral makeup of some people simply precludes a consistent and pervasive mental attitude of independence on their part.

14. Some CPA licensing rules and continuing professional education requirements mitigate this dilemma without eliminating it.

15. The SEC believes that auditor independence is fundamental in implementing the purposes of the Securities Acts.

16. SEC Accounting Series Release No. 126, "Guidelines and Examples of Situations Involving the Independence of Accountants," presents examples of situations impairing independence.

17. Rule 101 of the AICPA's Code of Professional Conduct covers independence requirements. Interpretation 101-9 defines effects of family relationships

Legal liability of auditors

1. Until the 1960s, auditor professional liability was limited to clients and others with a <u>direct</u> economic interest in audited financial statements.

2. Now third parties with only general interest in an auditor's work can also sue for
   - professional negligence
   - nonobservance of GAAP or GAAS
   - lack of due care in the conduct of an audit
   - association with misleading/fraudulent financial statements
   - lack of independence.

3. In the case of Bar Chris Construction Corporation (1968), although management distributed demonstrably incorrect information, the auditors were held liable because they had not made a reasonable effort to check the facts.

4. In the case of Continental Vending Machine Corporation illegal funds and other irregularities involving Continental's president were not properly reported in the audited financial statements; the case produced criminal convictions against some auditors.

5. In the ESM Government Securities case (1985) an audit partner pleaded guilty to fraud charges for receiving bribes from ESM officers and issuing unqualified opinions on ESM financial statements while knowing they were misleading and false. The auditor was sentenced to 12 years in prison; the audit firm was ordered to pay $70.9 million in damages to ESM creditors.

6. There appears to be a trend toward greater third-party responsibility for auditors.

7. Because CPAs are licensed and have a preferential economic position, users of audit services expect high quality audits.

8. User expectations do not always match realistic audit performance possibilities; lawsuits result.

Extensions of audit function

1. Auditor expertise is being extended from financial statements to other "attestation" services.

2. An attest engagement is one in which a practitioner is engaged to issue or does issue a written communication that expresses a conclusion about the reliability of a written assertion that is the responsibility of another party.

3. This development toward additional attestation services is reinforced by strong competition among audit firms and trends toward an overall service economy.

4. There are eleven attestation standards; these are extensions of GAAS, and they do not supersede GAAS.

5. Attestation engagements include, among others, such activities as
   - occupancy, enrollment, and attendance data,
   - labor data for union contract negotiations,
   - technical accuracy of college textbooks.

6. Another extension of the audit function is the social audit which concerns the social impact of business enterprises (pollution, use of natural resources, safety standards, etc.); such audits are required in France and strongly recommended in several other European countries.

Auditing in the public sector

1. The auditing profession is also extending its traditional boundaries in the public sector.

2. The General Accounting Office (GAO) is the auditing watchdog of the U.S. Congress.

3. The GAO is engaging increasingly in "performance" audits designed to determine the effectiveness of a particular agency or program management.

4. The GAO has published a body of audit standards applicable to all forms of governmental organizations and activities; these standards are intended to apply to government and private auditors alike when audit work is performed in the government sector.

5. Most large federal cabinet-level deparments and state governments maintain growing audit agencies of their own; their auditors typically have the power to publish their findings without jeopardy and are able to deliver their reports and recommendations to the highest management levels of the organizations they serve.

6. In some states the state auditor is elected and therefore subject to at least some influence from political pressures.

QUESTIONS AND EXERCISES

A. TRUE FALSE. Indicate whether each of the following statements is true or false.

_____ 14-1. The Securities and Exchange Commission issues CPA certificates.

_____ 14-2. The American Institute of Certified Public Accountants sets generally accepted auditing standards.

_____ 14-3. Auditors are responsible for the financial statements of their clients, and their reviews add credibility to those statements.

_____ 14-4. An unqualified audit report indicates that the auditor's job is to express an opinion on the financial statements.

_____14-5. An unqualified audit report indicates that GAAS require that the auditor obtain reasonable assurance as to whether the financial statements are free of material misstatement.

_____14-6. At the beginning of an audit, the auditor assumes that the GAAP utilized have been applied consistently between the current and prior periods.

_____14-7. At the beginning of the audit, the auditor assumes that there is adequate disclosure in the financial statements and footnotes.

_____14-8. Generally accepted auditing standards are set by the CPA profession itself.

_____14-9. An audit made in accordance with generally accepted auditing standards includes no procedures designed to detect material errors.

_____14-10. Board audit committees typically are comprised of outside directors (not corporate officers).

_____14-11. An attest engagement is one in which a practitioner is engaged to issue or does issue a written communication that expresses a conclusion about the reliability of a written assertion that is the responsibility of another party.

_____14-12. Performance audits are designed to determine the effectiveness of a particular agency or program management.

_____14-13. Although an independent CPA's auditing fees are paid by company managements, s/he owes primary professional allegiance to the investing public.

_____14-14. Most large business firms have well-organized internal audit departments. Internal auditors sometimes sign the auditor's reports published in corporate annual reports that are made available to shareholders and bankers.

_____14-15. A major function of the independent auditor is the detection of fraud.

___14-16. The independent auditor is not responsible for assuring, among other things, that the financial statements present fairly the operations of the business under audit.

B. MULTIPLE CHOICE. - Select the best response for each of the following, and mark the letter corresponding to your choice.

14-17. The auditor's opinion is unqualified when the following condition(s) is/are met:

   a. Accounting principles have been consistently applied.
   b. The financial statements have been prepared in accordance with generally accepted accounting principles.
   c. The audit examination was made in accordance with generally accepted auditing standards.
   d. b and c.
   e. a, b, and c.

14-18. Auditing is concerned with:

   a. Establishing generally accepted accounting principles.
   b. Guaranteeing the truth of the firm's financial statements.
   c. Choosing the accounting model underlying the preparation of the financial statements.
   d. The reliability or quality of the firm's disclosures.
   e. b and d.

14-19. The person(s) to whom the auditor's report is addressed is (are) usually:

   a. Company management.
   b. The SEC.
   c. The FASB.
   d. The company's major creditors.
   e. The Board of Directors and stockholders.

14-20. Auditor independence:

   a. Is implied if the auditor has no economic interest in the client.
   b. Is a question of fact, not appearance.
   c. Is a question of appearance, not fact.
   d. Is a question of fact and appearance.

14-21. The gathering of evidential matter in an audit is a result of:

   a. Tests.
   b. Selected observations.
   c. Statistical sampling.
   d. b and c.
   e. a, b, and c.

14-22. The receptionist at WWW Company prepares and mails all bank deposits as checks are received. The company's bookkeeper reconciles each monthly bank statement to the company's cash records. This segregation of employee responsibilities is a good example of:

   a. GAAS.
   b. GAAP.
   c. Internal controls.
   d. External controls.

14-23. In the U.S. the straight-line method of depreciation is an example of:

   a. FASB
   b. GAAS
   c. GAAP
   d. IASC

14-24. Which of the following best describes what is meant by generally accepted auditing standards?

   a. Acts to be performed by the auditor.
   b. Measures of the quality of the auditor's performance.
   c. Procedures to be used to gather evidence to support opinions on financial statements.
   d. Legal requirements applicable to individual audit engagements.
   e. Qualifications an individual must possess in order to become a CPA.

14-25. A CPA, while performing an audit, strives to achieve independence in appearance in order to :

a. Reduce risk and liability.
b. Maintain public confidence in the profession.
c. Become independent in fact.
d. Comply with laws and regulations administered by the SEC.
e. Work around the dilemma of receiving audit fees from the company being audited.

14-26. The general standards of generally accepted auditing standards include:

a. The audit is to be performed by a person or persons having adequate technical training and proficiency as an auditor.
b. A sufficient understanding of the internal control structure is to be obtained to plan the audit and to determine the nature, timing, and extent of tests to be performed.
c. Due professional care is to be exercised in the performance of the audit and the preparation of the report.
d. "a" and "c".
e. All of the above.

14-27. Generally accepted auditing standards of reporting include:

a. The report shall state whether the financial statements are prepared in accordance with generally accepted accounting principles.
b. The report shall identify those circumstances in which such principles have not been consistently observed in the current period in relation to the preceding period.
c. Due professional care is to be exercised in the performance of the audit and the preparation of the report.
d. All of the above.
e. "a" and "b".

14-28. The AICPA recommends that audit working papers show:

   a. data sufficient to demonstrate that the financial statements or other information upon which the auditor is reporting are in agreement with (or reconciled with) the client's record;
   b. how exceptions and unusual matters were resolved or treated;
   c. comments indicating the auditors' conclusions about significant aspects of the engagement.
   d. All of the above.
   e. "a" and "b".

14-29. It is management's responsibility to:

   a. comply with generally accepted accounting principles.
   b. comply with generally accepted auditing standards.
   c. safeguard enterprise assets.
   d. "a" and "c".
   e. All of the above.

14-30. Adverse opinions are issued if:

   a. there is <u>disagreement</u> with one or more aspects of the financial statements.
   b. the financial statements do not "present fairly" the financial position, results of operations and cash flows of a company.
   c. the auditor has not been able to obtain sufficient evidence.
   d. the financial statements are fundamentally impacted by uncertainty (e.g., a high probability of bankruptcy).
   e. All of the above.

14-31. Which statement is true regarding responsibility for the form and content of financial statements?

a. A CPA is responsible for issuing a "qualified report" when professional standards indicate the company qualifies to sell securities to the public.
b. Management has the responsibility to adopt internal controls necessary to assure that transactions are properly recorded.
c. CPAs have primary responsibility for financial statements, while management's role is secondary.
d. Financial statements are representations solely of the CPAs who render an opinion on them.
e. "b" and "c" are correct.

14-32. Which of the following is NOT a feature of an auditing framework?

a. The initial assumption that everything is "above board".
b. Review and examination of a firm's internal control system.
c. Examination of evidential matter.
d. Formulation of a judgmental opinion based on sampled evidence.
e. None of the above.

14-33. The objective of a typical audit examination of financial statements is:

a. To provide assurance to investors that all applicable laws have been observed.
b. To assure that fraud, resulting in material financial statement errors, has been detected.
c. The expression of an opinion on the fairness of the financial statements taken as a whole.
d. To determine that the financial statements are accurate.
e. To evaluate management's performance during the period under examination.

14-34. Which of the following is NOT typically stated in the auditor's opinion?

    a. Generally accepted auditing standards have been followed in conducting the audit.
    b. The financial statements fairly represent the firm's results of operations and financial position.
    c. Generally accepted accounting principles have been followed in preparing the financial statements.
    d. The financial statements are free of material misstatement.
    e. All of the above are stated in the auditor's opinion.

14-35. Use the following excerpt from an auditor's opinion report to answer the question:

We have audited the accompanying balance sheets of the WWW Company as of December 31, 19X8, and the related statements of income, retained earnings, and cash flows for the year then ended...
In our opinion, the financial statements referred to above present fairly, in all material respects, the financial position of the WWW Company...

What type of opinion is the auditor rendering in regards to WWW Company?

    a. Adverse.
    b. Certified.
    c. Disclaimer.
    d. Qualified.
    e. Unqualified.

14-36. Suppose you are the auditor of a small public company in 19X7. During the year, fire destroyed the company's administrative offices, including most of the accounting records and source documents that support the disclosures in the 19X7 financial statements. What type of audit opinion would you give?

    a. Unqualified.
    b. Disclaimer.
    c. Adverse.
    d. Certified.
    e. Qualified.

STUDY GUIDE ANSWERS

CHAPTER ONE

THE ROLE OF ACCOUNTING

1-1	T	1-2	F	1-3	T	1-4	T	1-5	F
1-6	T	1-7	T	1-8	T	1-9	T	1-10	T
1-11	F	1-12	T	1-13	F	1-14	T	1-15	F
1-16	H	1-17	G	1-18	D	1-19	I and B		
1-20	C	1-21	A	1-22	E	1-23	K	1-24	J
1-25	D	1-26	E	1-27	E	1-28	E	1-29	D
1-30	E	1-31	C	1-32	B	1-33	A	1-34	E
1-35	D								

CHAPTER TWO

PRESENT VALUE APPROACH TO INVESTMENT DECISIONS

2-1	B	2-2	C	2-3	D	2-4	A	2-5	F
2-6	E								

2-7　C　1,000 (5.56) = 5,560

2-8　B
$$
\begin{aligned}
40,000\,(1.21) &= 48,400 \\
40,000\,(1.10) &= 44,000 \\
40,000\,(1.00) &= \underline{40,000} \\
&\ 132,400
\end{aligned}
$$

2-9　D
$$
\begin{aligned}
(4,000)\,(1.4) &= 5,600 \\
(4,000)\,(1.25) &= \underline{5,000} \\
&\ 10,600
\end{aligned}
$$

2-10　A　30,000 (.621) = 18,630

2-11　D　2,000 (1.31) = 2,620
2-12　D　3,000 (.596) = 1,788

2-13　A
$$
\begin{aligned}
200\,(11.26) &= 2,252 \\
&\ \ \underline{-2,000} \\
&\ \ \ 252
\end{aligned}
$$

2-14   A   (-100.) (1) =   -100.00
                100. (.890 =   89.00
                100. (.840) =   84.00
                100. (.792) =   <u>79.20</u>
                                        $152.20

2-15   C   5000. (1) =   5,000
                5,000. (2.32) =   <u>11,600</u>
                                        16,600

2-16   A   (.621) (X) + (3.79) (2) = $47
                X = $63.48

2-17   C

2-18   B   (1,000) (X)= 2,000; X = 2; On the future value table look down
                the column for 15% until you locate a factor close to 2. Read
                across the row to the left side to find 5 periods.

2-19   D   500,000 (.8) =   40,000
                40,000 (8.36) =   <u>334,400</u>
                                        374,400

2-20   C   1/2.10 (1,000)

2-21   A   20,000 (5.08) =   101,600
                500,000 (.746)=   <u>373,000</u>
                                        <u>474,600</u>

2-22   D   7,000 = 2,000 X
                X = 3.5   On the present value of an annuity table read across
                the row for five periods to locate 3.5. It is between 12% and 14%.

2-23   A   (6.14) (X) = 10,000
                X = $1,628.66

2-24   C   Use 2% and 12 periods
                (1,000) (1.27) = $1,270

2-25   B
2-26   C   1,000
                (1,000) (3.17) =   <u>3,170</u>
                                        <u>4,170</u>

CHAPTER THREE

BASIC CONCEPTS AND INCOME DETERMINATION

3-1	J	3-2	D	3-3	I	3-4	A	3-5	B
3-6	E	3-7	H	3-8	C	3-9	K	3-10	L
3-11	F	3-12	M	3-13	N	3-14	G	3-15	F

3-16   120,000 + 15,000 change in accounts receivable = $135,000

3-17   10,000 + 25,000 + 2,000 + 40,000 +3,000 +300 +7,000 = $87,300

3-18   30,000 + 3,000 = $33,000

3-19 $4,000

3-20   120,000 + 15,000 + 30,000 + 3,000 = $168,000 cash inflows
        10,000 + 25,000 +2,000 +40,000 +3,000 +300 +7,000
                            +4,000 = $91,300 cash outflows
        168,000 Inflows - 91,300 outflows = $76,700 net cash increase

3-21   120,000 + 30,000 = 150,000

3-22   10,000 + 25,000 +40,000 + 13,000 +5,000 +300 = 93,300

3-23   150,000 - 93,300 + 1,000 gain on sale =$ 57,700

3-24   57,700 -7,000 = $50,700

3-25	C	3-26	C	3-27	C	3-28	C	3-29	B
3-30	C	3-31	E	3-32	A	3-33	D	3-34	E
3-35	A	3-36	C	3-37	A	3-38	E	3-39	D
3-40	E	3-41	D	3-42	E	3-43	B	3-44	E
3-45	E	3-46	E	3-47	E	3-48	E	3-49	E
3-50	E	3-51	E	3-52	C	3-53	A	3-54	E
3-55	A	3-56	E	3-57	C	3-58	C	3-59	C
3-60	E	3-61	C	3-62	E	3-63	C	3-64	E
3-65	E	3-66	A	3-67	E	3-68	D	3-69	B
3-70	C								

3-71   D   9,500 + 100 = 9,600

3-72   D   5,000 + 2,000 +6,000 +800 = 13,800

3-73　C　10,000 + 10,000 = 20,000

3-74　A　　　3-75　E

3-76　C　10,000 - 100 - 4,400 - 2,000 - 100 = 3,400

3-77　A　3,400 - 1,000 = 2,400

3-78　A　　　3-79　C　　　3-80　A　　　3-81　D

CHAPTER FOUR

BASIC CONCEPTS AND BALANCE SHEET MEASURES

4-1　D　　　4-2　B

4-3　C　45,000 - 6,000 = 39,000

4-4　B　Beginning Owners' Equity + New Paid-in capital + Net income
- Dividends = Ending Owners' Equity

0 + PIC + 7,000 - 1,000 = 15,000 ; PIC = 9,000

4-5　E　15,000 + net income - 5,000 + 2,000 = 39,000
NI = 27,000

4-6　A　39,000 + 16,000 - 2,000 +1,000 = 54,000
Assets - Liabilities = Owners' Equity
Assets - 9,000 = 54,000 ; Assets = 63,000

4-7　C　120 months ÷ 24 = $5 per month;　8 months X $5 = $40

4-8　D

4-9　C　240 - 36 = 204

4-10　B

4-11　E　2,000 - 500 -240 -120 + 5 + 900 = 2,045

4-12　B　0 + 2,000 + 9 - Dividends = 2,009

4-13　E　　　4-14　A　　　4-15　A　　　4-16　E　　　4-17　C

4-18 A $18,000 + 64,000 - 10,000 = 72,000$

4-19 C

4-20 B $X + 130,000 - 50,000 = 190,000;\ X = 110,000$

4-21 B Assets - Liabilities = Owners' Equity
Beginning of Year: $80,000 - 60,000 = 20,000$
By end of year:
Liabilities $= 60,000 + 30,000 = 90,000$
Assets $- 90,000 = 20,000 + 40,000$; Assets $= 150,000$
Increase during year: $150,000 - 80,000 = 70,000$

4-22 D

4-23 D $1,000 + P - 4,000 = 3,000$; $P = 6,000$

4-24 C

4-25 B (See solution to 4-21)
$110,000 - 80,000 = 30,000$
$80,000 - 15,000 = 65,000$ Liabilities
Beginning Owners' Equity
+ New Paid-in capital
+ net income
- Dividends
Ending Owners' Equity
$30,000 + 0 + 45,000 - 0 = 75,000$
End of Year: Assets - Liabilities = Owners' Equity
Assets $- 65,000 = 75,000$; Assets $= 140,000$
Change: $140,000 - 110,000 = 30,000$

| 4-26 | C | 4-27 | D | 4-28 | E | 4-29 | E | 4-30 | C |
| 4-31 | F | 4-32 | I | 4-33 | G | 4-34 | H | | |

CHAPTER FIVE

STATEMENT OF CASH FLOWS

5-1	F	5-2	T	5-3	T	5-4	T	5-5	T
5-6	T	5-7	F	5-8	T	5-9	T	5-10	F
5-11	T	5-12	F	5-13	T	5-14	C	5-15	B
5-16	C	5-17	B	5-18	D	5-19	D	5-20	D
5-21	A	5-22	E						

5-23 C $25,000 + X - 165,000 = 37,500$; $X = 177,500$

5-24 B $375 + 2,100 - 175 = 2,300$

5-25 D $2,500 + 83,000 - 4,000 = 81,500$

5-26 B Sales - increase in accounts receivable
$480 - 100 = 380$

5-27 C Cost of goods sold - decrease in inventory + decrease in AP
$90 - 20 + 50 = 120$

5-28 C Wages expense - change in wages payable
$90 - 20 = 70$

5-29 A Advertising expense: 30

5-30 B Depreciation does not involve cash flow.

5-31 D Rent expense - decrease in prepaid rent
$15 - 5 = 10$

5-32 B Interest expense + decrease in interest payable
$8 + 2 = 10$

5-33 B (From answers to 4-26 through 4-32)
$380 - 120 - 70 - 30 - 10 - 10 = 140$

5-34 B Equipment: $700 - 600 = 100$ outflow

5-35 D $300 - 250 = 50$ outflow

5-36 C $685 - 485 = 200$ inflow

5-37 B Beginning retained earnings + Net income - Dividends =
Ending Retained Earnings
$0 + 167 - D = 117$; Dividends = 50

5-38 A (From 4-35 through 4-37)
$-50 + 200 - 50 = 100$

5-39   A   Change in cash account: 290 - 150 = 140
            Operations: 140
            Investing   -100
            Financing   100
            Net change   140

5-40   B   Net income   167
            - increase in accounts receivable   -100
            + decrease in inventory   20
            + decrease in prepaid rent   5
            - decrease in accounts payable   -50
            + increase in wages payable   20
            - decrease in interest payable   -2
            + depreciation   80
            cash flow   140

5-41   B   Equipment: $100 outflow

5-42   D   Mortgage payable: $50 outflow

5-43   C   Change in paid-in capital; 685 - 485 = $200 inflow.

5-44   B   Beginning retained earnings
            + net income
            - dividends
            Ending retained earnings

            0 + 167 - D = 117; D = 50

5-45   A   See answers to numbers 42-44.
            - 50 + 200 - 50 = 100

5-46   A   Change in cash account: 290 - 150 = 140

            Operations: 140
            Investing   - 100
            Financing   100
            Change   140

CHAPTER SIX

ACCOUNTING FOR THE EFFECTS OF CHANGING PRICES

6-1	T	6-2	F	6-3	F	6-4	T	6-5	F
6-6	T	6-7	T	6-8	T	6-9	F	6-10	T

220

6-11	F	6-12	F	6-13	F	6-14	T	6-15	T
6-16	A	6-17	A	6-18	A	6-19	C		

6-20   E   Supplies are NONmonetary.

6-21   A

6-22   D

1,000	(120/100)	=	1,200
2,200	(120/110)	=	2,400
-1,980	(120/110)	=	-2,160
150		=	150
1,370			1,590

1,590. - 1,370 = 220 loss

2,000   (120/100)   =   2,400

2,400. - 2,000   = 400 gain

400. gain - 220 loss = $180 gain

6-23   D

6-24   C   decrease in net monetary assets results in gain
10,000   (121/110) =   11,000

11,000. - 10,000 = 1,000 gain

6-25	B	6-26	A	6-27	C	6-28	C	6-29	C
6-30	C	6-31	B						

6-32   C $10,000 ÷ 5,000 = $2 historical cost per game

Current cost of asset
- historical cost of asset
Unrealized holding gain

$3 - $2 = $1 gain per unit; $1 (5,000 units) = $5,000

6-33   A

6-34   C   300.   (110/105)= $314.28

6-35   B   51,000.   (110/100) = 56,100

6-36   B   1,800.   (110/100) = 1,980

CHAPTER SEVEN

THE FINANCIAL ACCOUNTING INFORMATION SYSTEM

7-1	T	7-2	T	7-3	F	7-4	F	7-5	F
7-6	T	7-7	F	7-8	T	7-9	F	7-10	F
7-11	F	7-12	F	7-13	F	7-14	T		

7-15   B   15,000 - 10,000 + 20,000 + 49,000 - 25,000 - 11,000 - 8,000 + 12,000 - 5,000 = 37,000

7-16   C   20,000. + 55,000 - 49,000 = 26,000

7-17   E   5,000. + 30,000 - 28,000 = 7,000

7-18   C

40,000.	+	10,000.	=	50,000
-20,000.		-7,000		-27,000
20,000.	+	3,000	=	23,000

7-19   A   13,500.   +   30,000   -   25,000   =   18,500

7-20	C	35,000	+	12,000	=	47,000
7-21	C	20,000	+	55,000	=	75,000

7-22   A   17,000. + 28,000 + 3,000 + 7,000 = 55,000

7-23   C   0 + 8,000 - 3,000 = 5,000

7-24   B   0 + 6,000 = 6,000

7-25   D

Beginning retained earnings		11,500
+ Revenues	75,000	
- Expenses	-55,000	
Net income		20,000
- Dividends		-5,000
Ending retained earnings		26,500

7-26	A	7-27	B	7-28	A	7-29	B	7-30	C
7-31	A	7-32	B	7-33	A				

7-34	C	Beginning balance	1,000 @ 500	500,000
		Purchases	200 @ 500	100,000
		Available		600,000
		Cost of goods sold	500 @ 500	250,000
		Ending inventory	700 @ 500	350,000

7-35	D	Revenues	400,000
		Cost of pianos	-250,000
		Other expenses	-48,900
		Depreciation	-3,500
			97,600

CHAPTER EIGHT

REVENUE RECOGNITION AND MEASUREMENT ISSUES

8-1	F	8-2	T	8-3	F	8-4	T	8-5	T
8-6	T	8-7	T	8-8	T	8-9	F	8-10	F
8-11	T	8-12	T	8-13	T	8-14	F	8-15	F
8-16	T	8-17	T	8-18	T	8-19	T	8-20	F
8-21	T	8-22	T	8-23	T	8-24	T	8-25	T
8-26	T	8-27	T						

8-28 B 105,000 - 80,000 - 2,000 = 23,000

8-29	C	Allowance:	105,000 X 3% =	3,150
		Write-offs:		-2,000
		Balance		1,150
		Accounts receivable:		23,000
		Allowance		-1,150
		Net		21,850

8-30 B 105,000 X 3% = 3,150

8-31 D See solution to number 29.

8-32 D Revenues   28,000,000
         Estimated costs   21,000,000
         Estimated profit 7,000,000

         Year 1: 6,000,000/21,000,000 (7,000,000) =   2,000,000.

         Year 2: 18,000,000/21,000,000 (7,000,000)=   6,000,000.
                  Less profit recognized in Year 1:   -2,000,000.
                  Profit recognized in Year 2:   4,000,000

8-33 B $14,000,000 + $6,000,000 = $20,000,000

8-34 A Sales price   10,000
         Cost of sales   5,000
         Potential profit   5,000

         5,000 (6,000/10,000) = 3,000

8-35 D Total cash received during period   11,000
         Cost of sales   10,000
         Realized income   1,000

8-36 D No financing revenue has been earned at December 31
         as the sale was made the last day of the year.

8-37 B Present value at date of sale   4,169
         Down payment   -1,000
                                                  3,169

         3,169 X 10% = $317 financing revenue

8-38 D Total price   495
         without warranty   -345
         Price of warranty   150

CHAPTER NINE

ASSET MEASUREMENT AND EXPENSE RECOGNITION

9-1	T	9-2	T	9-3	T	9-4	T	9-5	T
9-6	T	9-7	F	9-8	F	9-9	T	9-10	T
9-11	T	9-12	F	9-13	T	9-14	F	9-15	T
9-16	F	9-17	T	9-18	T	9-19	F	9-20	F
9-21	T	9-22	T	9-23	T	9-24	F	9-25	T
9-26	T	9-27	T	9-28	T	9-29	F	9-30	T

9-31 F   9-32   F   9-33   T   9-34   T   9-35   T
9-36 T

9-37 C   36,000 - 4,000 = 32,000
              4 + 3 + 2 + 1 = 10
              32,000 (4/10) = 12,800

9-38 D   See solution to number 37.
              32,000 (3/10) = 9,600

9-39 A   36,000 - 4,000 = 32,000
              32,000 ÷ 16,000 = $2 per unit
              6,000 X $2 = $12,000

9-40 B   Straight-line rate for four year life is 25% per year.
              25 % doubled = 50%
              36,000 X 50% = 18,000

9-41 D   See solution to number 40.
              36,000 - 18,000 = 18,000
              18,000 X 50% = 9,000

9-42 D   See solutions to number 40 and 41.

Cost	36,000
Depreciation - year 1	-18,000
Depreciation - year 2	-9,000
Book value	9,000
Sales price	8,000
Book value	-9,000
Loss on sale	-1,000

9-43 C | | |
              |---|---|
              | 100 @ 10 | 1,000 |
              | 10 @ 11 | 110 |
              | | 1,110 |

9-44 C | | |
              |---|---|
              | 100 @ 14 | 1,400 |
              | 300 @ 13 | 3,900 |
              | 490 @ 11 | 5,390 |
              | | 10,690 |

225

9-45	D	100 @ 10	1,000
		500 @ 11	5,500
		300 @ 13	3,900
		100 @ 14	1,400
		1,000	11,800

$$11,800 \div 1,000 = \$11,80$$

$$110 \times \$11.80 = \$1,298$$

9-46 A See solution to number 45.
1,000 - 110 = 890 units sold.
890 ($11.80) = $10,502

9-47	B	100 @ 14 =	1,400
		10 @ 13 =	130
			1,530

9-48	A	100 @ 10	1,000
		500 @ 11	5,500
		290 @ 13	3,770
			10,270

CHAPTER TEN

LIABILITY MEASUREMENT AND EXPENSE RECOGNITION

10-1	F	10-2	T	10-3	T	10-4	T	10-5	F
10-6	F	10-7	F	10-8	F	10-9	F	10-10	T
10-11	T	10-12	T	10-13	F	10-14	F	10-15	F
10-16	T	10-17	F	10-18	F	10-19	T	10-20	T
10-21	T	10-22	F	10-23	F	10-24	F	10-25	T
10-26	T	10-27	T	10-28	T	10-29	T	10-30	F
10-31	T	10-32	F	10-33	F	10-34	T	10-35	F
10-36	T	10-37	F	10-38	T	10-39	T	10-40	T
10-41	T	10-42	T	10-43	F	10-44	T	10-45	F
10-46	T	10-47	T	10-48	T	10-49	T	10-50	T
10-51	T	10-52	T	10-53	F	10-54	A	10-55	A

10-56 C 50,000 - 3,790 = 46,210

10-57 A 50,000 X 8% = 4,000

10-58 C 46,210 X 10% = 4,621

10-59 C See solutions to numbers 57 and 58.

First period interest expense   4,621
Cash paid   4,000
Discount to amortize   621

3,790 - 621 = 3,169

50,000 - 3,169 = 46,831

10-60 D   46,831 X 10% = 4,683

CHAPTER ELEVEN

RECOGNITION OF OWNERSHIP INTERESTS

11-1	T	11-2	T	11-3	T	11-4	T	11-5	T
11-6	F	11-7	T	11-8	T	11-9	F	11-10	F
11-11	T	11-12	T	11-13	T	11-14	T	11-15	T
11-16	T	11-17	T	11-18	T	11-19	F	11-20	T
11-21	F	11-22	F	11-23	T	11-24	T	11-25	T
11-26	T	11-27	T	11-28	T	11-29	T	11-30	T
11-31	T	11-32	F	11-33	F	11-34	F	11-35	T
11-36	T	11-37	T	11-38	T	11-39	T	11-40	T
11-41	F	11-42	T	11-43	T	11-44	T	11-45	T
11-46	C	11-47	A	11-48	B	11-49	D	11-50	D
11-51	B	11-52	E	11-53	E	11-54	E		

CHAPTER TWELVE

POLICY MAKING

12-1	T	12-2	T	12-3	T	12-4	F	12-5	T
12-6	T	12-7	F	12-8	T	12-9	D	12-10	T
12-11	F	12-12	T	12-13	F	12-14	F	12-15	T
12-16	F	12-17	F	12-18	T	12-19	T	12-20	T
12-21	T	12-22	F	12-23	T	12-24	F	12-25	T
12-26	T	12-27	T	12-28	T	12-29	F	12-30	F
12-31	T	12-32	T	12-33	F	12-34	F	12-35	F
12-36	T	12-37	T	12-38	T	12-39	T	12-40	T
12-41	T	12-42	T	12-43	T	12-44	T	12-45	T
12-46	F	12-47	T	12-48	T	12-49	F	12-50	T
12-51	F	12-52	T	12-53	T	12-54	T	12-55	T
12-56	T	12-57	T	12-58	T	12-59	F	12-60	F

CHAPTER THIRTEEN

FINANCIAL REPORTING AND ANALYSIS

13-1	F	13-2	T	13-3	F	13-4	F	13-5	F
13-6	F	13-7	T	13-8	F	13-9	T	13-10	T
13-11	T	13-12	T	13-13	F	13-14	F	13-15	T
13-16	T	13-17	F	13-18	F	13-19	F	13-20	F
13-21	T	13-22	T	13-23	T	13-24	T	13-25	T
13-26	F	13-27	T	13-28	T	13-29	F	13-30	T
13-31	T	13-32	F	13-33	T	13-34	T	13-35	T
13-36	T	13-37	T	13-38	F	13-39	T	13-40	T
13-41	T	13-42	T	13-43	F	13-44	F	13-45	F
13-46	F	13-47	F	13-48	F	13-49	F	13-50	F
13-51	F	13-52	F	13-53	F	13-54	T	13-55	T
13-56	F	13-57	T	13-58	F	13-59	F	13-60	F
13-61	T	13-62	T	13-63	F	13-64	T		

13-65 A $167 \div 500 = \$.334$

13-66 A $[167 + 8] \div [(970 + 1{,}205) \div 2] = 16.1$

13-67 A $[167] \div [(485 + 802) \div 2] = 26\%$

13-68 C $167 \div 480 = 34.8\%$

13-69 D $(290 + 200 + 230 + 15) \div (125 + 20 + 8) = 4.8$

13-70 B $(290 + 200 + 15) \div (125 + 20 + 8) = 3.3$

13-71 B $(125 + 20 + 8 + 250) \div 1{,}205 = 33.4\%$

13-72 A $(167 + 8) \div 8 = 21.9$

CHAPTER 14

AUDITING

14-1	F	14-2	T	14-3	F	14-4	T	14-5	T
14-6	T	14-7	T	14-8	T	14-9	F	14-10	T
14-11	T	14-12	T	14-13	T	14-14	F	14-15	F
14-16	F	14-17	E	14-18	D	14-19	E	14-20	D
14-21	E	14-22	C	14-23	C	14-24	B	14-25	B
14-26	D	14-27	E	14-28	D	14-29	D	14-30	B

14-31   B   14-32   E   14-33   C   14-34   E   14-35   E
14-36   B